POLITICAL DEMOGRAPHY, DEMOGRAPHIC ENGINEERING

Myron Weiner

and

Michael S. Teitelbaum

Berghahn Books
NEW YORK • OXFORD

Published in 2001 by

Berghahn Books

www.berghahnbooks.com

Library of Congress Cataloging-in-Publication Data
Weiner, Myron.
  Political demography, demographic engineering / by Myron Weiner,
  Michael Teitelbaum.
      p.   cm.
  Includes bibliographical references and index.
  ISBN 1-57181-253-9 — ISBN 1-57181-254-7 (alk. paper)
    1. Emigration and immigration—Political aspects. 2. Popula-
  tion geography—Political aspects. 3 Internal security.
  4. Security, international. I. Teitelbaum, Michael. II. Title.

  JV6477.W44   2001
  304.6—dc21   00-045546

British Library Cataloguing in Publication Data

A catalogue record for this book is available from
the British Library.

Printed in the United States on acid-free paper

CONTENTS

FOREWORD

The origins of this jointly written book lie in a phone call I received from Myron Weiner in April 1999. I knew, much to my dismay, that four months earlier he had been diagnosed with an aggressive brain tumor, and I understood from a mutual friend that it was inoperable and likely to prove fatal. I also knew that he had been undergoing radiation treatments and chemotherapy to slow the course of the disease, and that during a hiatus from such treatments he had undertaken a trip to South Africa, something that he had always wanted to do and which fulfilled a long-deferred promise to his wife, Sheila.

What I did not know until that April call is that, every morning since January at his home in Vermont, he had been working on a series of essays on political demography, a field that he had pioneered three decades earlier. Myron told me that he had hoped to be able to complete a substantial book on this topic, but by April he was finding that he could no longer write. He asked me if I would be willing to read the partial essays he had completed, and to give him comments. I readily agreed, and did so expeditiously. I told him that six of the seven essays, though incomplete, were vintage Myron Weiner: insightful, incisive, creative, and provocative.

A week or so later, Myron's son, Saul, called me to say that his father was not able to talk on the phone, but had asked him to contact me and see if I would be willing to consider taking the essays as the skeleton and partial body of a jointly authored book on political demography and demographic engineering. I expressed some hesitation on grounds that Myron might not be able to review the parts that I would author, but his son said that Myron had anticipated such a concern, and had indicated that he knew from our previous joint writing that he would find my analyses and writing style perfectly consistent with his own.

Myron Weiner died before I was able to turn my efforts to this volume. Writing it has been an experience at once poignant and exhilarating—poignant to be writing a joint volume embodying the unfinished work of an extraordinary scholar, exhilarating to be working with material so full of intellectual honesty and insight.

Myron Weiner's departure has deprived us of the world's leading political scientist on matters demographic. Perversely, it has done so at the very time that the political dimensions of population change are increasingly being seen as central to the agendas of presidents, premiers, legislators, and other political leaders in many countries. Yet such concerns often are expressed in emotional, ideological, and ill-informed ways. I am confident that Myron would join me in expressing the hope that this volume might stimulate others to address the political dimensions of demographic change in ways that embody the care and objectivity they deserve.

Michael S. Teitelbaum

PREFACE

Over the past decade, the impacts of demographic trends on international security and on peaceful relations between and within states have come to the fore in ways not seen since the aftermath of World War II. An evolving and more complex set of concerns over population has become the basis for a new look at the security effects of changes in the size, distribution, and composition of populations. This book is an attempt to lay out this new look, to take issue with some of the prevailing views on the political consequences of population change, and to suggest where the concerns are realistic and where they are not.

My initial interest in what I have called "political demography" began in the early 1970s when I undertook a study of the costs and benefits of migration to the local inhabitants of places in India to which migrants moved. Indian policy makers faced a genuine dilemma in the precise sense of a situation requiring a choice between two undesirables. On the one hand, providing special protection to some ethnic group meant denying equal opportunities to others, while on the other hand, not acting meant permitting the resentment of local people to fester. How to find a way in which local people belonging to one ethnic community could obtain greater equality in the employment market without at the same time restricting the opportunities of migrants and their descendants belonging to other ethnic groups seemed to be an intractable problem, for India as for other multiethnic societies.

While I was conducting research for that study (Weiner 1978), I was asked by Roger Revelle of Harvard's Center for Population Studies, then Foreign Secretary of the National Academy of Sciences, to participate in a major National Academy study of the consequences and policy implications of rapid population growth. Revelle was eager to include in the project a state-of-the-art paper on whether population density and rapid population growth accounted for many of the disturbing features of a changing world: urban violence, political instability, and aggressive behavior. It clearly mattered politically that populations in developing countries were becoming younger, that population growth puts strains on the capacity of administrative systems to provide services, that structural strains were growing in relationships within families and within communities, and that migration within and between countries was on the rise. As a political scientist I was drawn to these questions, notwithstanding the difficulties of separating out demographic determinants from the many other factors that were shaping political outcomes.

My work on the political effects of migration within India led me to think more critically about the effects of migration elsewhere and to take a less rosy view of migration than the one found in American social science writings. By the early 1990s it had become clear than unwanted and illegal international migration and an increase in refugee flows were a significant threat to many states and communities, and that neither individual governments nor the "international community" had any ready solutions. Migration and refugee issues had become foreign and domestic policy issues for the United States and for very many other countries.

With support from the Sloan Foundation, I organized a conference on international migration and security at the MIT Center for International Studies in December 1991. The conference and the resulting book (Weiner 1993) attracted positive attention from my colleagues in the field of security studies, but not among those who worked on refugee issues, who turned their attention to the normative questions of human rights. Indeed, for a while there was tension between those who looked at refugee issues through human rights lenses and those who saw it from a security perspective, a dichotomy which I did not regard as particularly helpful.

In collaboration with the American Assembly, Michael S. Teitelbaum of the Sloan Foundation and I organized a conference on "World Migration and U.S. Policy," which resulted in the publication of *Threatened Peoples, Threatened Borders* (1995), a volume which sought to call attention to the ways in which the influx of refugees, asylum seekers, and other international migrants had become both a major humanitarian challenge and a threat to the national and international security of states. In 1995, with generous support from the MacArthur Foundation, I wrote *The Global Migration Crisis: Challenge to States and to Human Rights.* The volume analyzed how governments and their citizens viewed these flows, how they were responding to demands for entry by would-be migrants and refugees, and—what was becoming a major foreign policy issue in one country after another—how governments and international organizations could change the conditions within states that produced refugees and illegal migrants.

The essays in the present volume are an effort to further our understanding of the political consequences of population change. I am pleased to acknowledge the support of the Smith Richardson Foundation for making these essays possible. The Foundation provided support for a workshop held at MIT in December 1998 at which commissioned papers were presented focusing on both sides of the relationship between demography and security—how demography shaped security and how in turn security concerns led governments to try to affect demography.

I began writing the essays in this volume in early January 1999, four weeks after I was diagnosed with glioblastoma, an aggressive inoperable brain tumor. The reason for informing the reader is not to seek indulgence for errors of fact or poor judgment that are sure to appear in these essays, but rather to explain why I have worked under more than usual time constraints, uncertain as to how my malady would affect my writing, but also mindful of Samuel Johnson's quip about the effects of anticipating one's own hanging. Johnson also wrote, I reminded myself, that a man may write at any time if he will set himself doggedly to it.

Myron Weiner died at his home in Vermont on June 3, 1999.

INTRODUCTION

Population—its growth or decline, its movement, its density, its characteristics, its distribution—has always been linked to questions of security. The movement of peoples has made and unmade states, and transformed societies. Population growth has been regarded as a source of national power or, alternatively, as a contributor to disorder and violence. The subject long ago captured the concerted attention of ancient and classical political philosophers and commentators. Yet, perhaps surprisingly, it is one that has been little attended by modern commentators on international relations and politics.[1]

There has been a waxing and waning of popular interest in population issues as a factor in human security, and what constitutes the population "problem" has been redefined from one generation to the next, and differs from one country to another. For much of the twentieth century, population has been treated as part of a dystopic vision, as in one way or another undermining the well-being of individuals, the communities in which they live, and the states which govern them. This perspective has long since become more complex and nuanced than the subsistence concerns of Malthus; indeed, much of the Malthusian analysis has been discredited as a consequence of extraordinary increases in the production of food, and of our capacity both to exploit and transform our environment. In the post-Cold War world, population-related issues once again loom large as a potential source of disorder—along with terrorism, global warming, the threat of weapons of mass destruction, civil violence and ethnic conflict, the spread of drugs and pathogens, and attacks against global telecommunications.

This book considers some of the most striking of the rapidly evolving connections between demographics and the security of both states and human groups within them. In so doing, we wish to advance three broad generalizations:

The first is that the past century has been one of the greatest demographic turbulence. For much of Europe after World War I, the population problem was defined as demographic growth that was too slow to sustain national security and economic prosperity. By the 1950s, such concerns had waned as the postwar "baby boom" developed in some (though not all) of these countries. Yet at the same time there were growing perceptions of explosive rates of demographic increase emerging in the formerly colonial regions of what is now called the "South" or the "developing world." The concern was that demographic growth in these regions was too rapid to maintain internal and international comity and to allow the attainment of economic prosperity.

By the mid-1960s, the high fertility rates of the "baby boom" in Western countries had begun to decline, but rising interest in environmental problems coupled with continuing rapid demographic increase in the South evoked a number of books with sensational titles such as "The Population Bomb." A decade further on, as clear signs appeared of accelerating fertility in the South, new alarms arose as fertility in the West declined to very low levels, thereby coming full circle with similar alarums during the 1930s. Meanwhile, the number of refugees in need of assistance rose dramatically, and immigration from abroad into low-fertility countries rose rapidly if sometimes erratically.

For some influential Americans, rapid domestic population growth since the 1950s has been seen as evidence of progress, for others as a driver of declining quality of life. Similarly, some Americans have seen increasing immigration as a source of national vitality and diversity, others as an economic drag and a threat to national integrity. In short, the past century has been a period of dramatic changes, unanticipated reversals, and frequent crosscurrents in both global and national demographic trends. These shifts and crosscurrents have in turn produced a noisy chorus of rhetoric, and a turbulent set of contending political responses and concerns.

The second generalization we wish to advance is that demographics have now emerged visibly into the realm of actions by states and other political actors seeking political advantage over, or protection from, their competitors. In some senses this is not a new phenomenon; after all, larger populations have long been sought by absolutist monarchs as instruments of their military and economic power, and expulsions or exterminations of groups perceived to threaten state power are hardly late twentieth-century innovations. Yet the very magnitudes of global and regional populations, their historically high growth rates, and the volumes of human migration movements since World War II do suggest that fundamental shifts are underway.

The third and final generalization is that these recent demographic patterns pose significant challenges to those concerned with developments in the realms of politics and security. This may be true, if only in a partial way, with respect to the impacts of very low and very high fertility rates. But it is powerfully consistent with recent reality with respect to international migration movements. Increasingly, states see large-scale international migratory movements toward their borders as representing threats to their security. Control over such entry is universally seen as central to state sovereignty, and states generally are seeking new instruments—unilateral, bilateral, and multilateral alike—to control unwanted migrations. Unfortunately, extant theories of international migration do not provide adequate explanations of the complex of forces that underlie such movements, and most migration theorists pay surprisingly scant attention to the impact of state actions regarding migration.

A brief explanation of the structure of this volume may be helpful. The first four chapters deal with overall demographic trends—driven by fertility, mortality, and migration—insofar as they have implications for state power, internal politics, external competition, and perhaps aggression.

Chapters 5 through 7 consider the roles played by states in "engineering" the addition or subtraction of human groups residing within their territory, including actions of recent concern such as "ethnic cleansing." They also deal with emerging patterns such as migrants' political mobilization against regimes in their countries of origin and the growth of dual nationality, both of which may further complicate the politics surrounding demographic patterns.

Chapters 8 and 9 focus on two different theoretical traditions addressing international migration: economic and social theories as the forces underlying such movements; and international relations/security theories addressing migrations as perceived threats.

Chapter 10 considers, in summary, whether claims that "demography is destiny" ought to be taken seriously. To what extent do the powerful demographic forces of fertility and migration drive political changes, or determine economic trends? And, perhaps more importantly, to what degree are such demographic forces immutable—too powerful for mere mortals to affect—or to what extent are they subject to control or at least modification by concerted state action?

The past century has indeed been one of powerful crosscurrents and passionate controversy about demographic trends. Looking forward, current demographic patterns and perceivable trends suggest more of the same, increasingly in ways that pose challenges to the securities of individuals, minority groups, nations, and states. It is our hope that the discussions in this volume will contribute to a reversal in the surprising inattention to such matters by modern commentators on international relations and politics. The humanity and effectiveness of actions by states, and the well-being of countless millions of threatened people, could benefit greatly from their thoughts and insights.

Note

1. For a recent symposium volume on this subject, see Weiner and Russell (2001).

— One —

GLOBAL DEMOGRAPHIC TRENDS AND THEIR SECURITY IMPLICATIONS

━━◗ʘ/ʘ/ʘ◖━━

Demographic visions of the future have rarely been benign. Few scholars or journalists have regarded the worldwide growth in population kindly. To be sure, a handful of writers have applauded the dramatic postwar expansion of populations (see, for example, Wattenberg 1987; Simon 1981), but in the main scholars and journalists have regarded population growth as a global burden. One need only look at the title of articles and books, from Ehrlich's 1968 best-seller, *The Population Bomb*, to recent writings on the world's carrying capacity. Such demographic visions are decidedly dystopic. By this we mean visions of the future in which demographic variables—rapid population growth, increased population density, high rates of uncontrollable migration—are regarded as having destructive consequences for social order, the functioning of government, relations among people, and national and individual security.

There have, of course, always been gloomy, even apocalyptic, anticipations of the future. In the nineteenth and early parts of the twentieth century both the utopian and dystopian visions centered on technology. But while the technology-based dystopia envisioned an ordered world in which human emotions were repressed and individuals were under the control of autocratic rulers—Huxley's *Brave New World* and Orwell's vision of

1984—the demographic dystopias envision a world that is chaotic, violent, and unpredictable.

Dystopias and utopias are imagined out of the present: The future is already with us, but not fully developed; the worst—or in the vision of utopias, the best—is yet to come. Our vision of the future is thus in part empirical, part imaginary. The technology-based dystopias emphasize our capacity to destroy ourselves by unwisely manipulating our genetic environment, employing weapons of mass destruction, fouling our air and water. The demography-based dystopias are about what Others can do to us, what threats they create in the form of terrorism, biological pathogens, drugs, and the cruelties that people commit upon themselves, drawn in by civil strife and genocide.

Demography-based dystopias also alert us to the threats created by others, not as a consequence of their strength but as a result of their weaknesses. From this perspective, genocide, ethnic warfare, famine, the spread of pathogens put us (in the West) at risk because of the ease with which Bad Things readily cross international borders. Moreover, for the West, the breakdown of social order elsewhere in the world poses a set of moral questions about the efficacy, risk, and obligations of doing something.

Another feature of the demographic dystopic model is that it is global, not national: Population growth is seen as running up against the world's carrying capacity; environmental degradation is worsened by population growth that poisons our atmosphere; forests destroyed by population growth deprive us of our oxygen; pathogens, made worse by crowding and poverty, enter our bloodstreams; and ethnic hatreds lead to violence and the flight of refugees across international borders.

The centerpiece of the demography-based dystopian models is that we are now experiencing a worldwide shift in population distribution, from the West to the Rest, that has implications for the well-being and security of the world's industrial democracies.[1] This shift has been well under way throughout this century and, so the argument goes, it will accelerate in the twenty-first century in ways that may well put the Western democracies at risk economically and militarily. In this section, we explore this argument, first with a brief account of global demographic trends, and then with a consideration of their potential consequences for the security and well-being of developed countries.

Imagine a world in which low-income countries had doubled or even tripled their populations in four decades. What would

the world look like—from a security and stability point of view—
if the populations of Turkey, South Africa, China, India, Bangladesh, Mexico, Indonesia, Ethiopia, Vietnam, the Philippines,
Brazil, and Egypt had doubled or more, and still other large
countries, Iran, Algeria, Nigeria, Pakistan, and Sudan had tripled
their populations? Imagine a world in which the population doubled and in which the share of the world's population that lived
in the industrial world declined from 31 percent to 20 percent in
forty years. Imagine the outcome if the population of sub-Saharan Africa, the world's poorest region with the highest rate of
population growth, had tripled and its share of world population
had increased from 7 to 10 percent.

We are, of course, describing what actually happened between
1960 and the estimated population in the year 2000. The future, as
it were, has arrived. According to the "medium-variant" of the
United Nations projections (United Nations 1999), the world population would further increase by nearly 50 percent by 2050, to 8.9
billion; the parallel "low-variant" projection for 2050 yields 7.3
billion, while the "high-variant" shows 10.7 billion. (Giving such
a range, from 7.3 to 10.7 billion, provides the reader a useful perspective as to the profound uncertainties of such long-range projections.) Using the same UN projections, the population of
sub-Saharan Africa would more than double, from 640 million to
1.5 billion (with a low-to-high range of 1.3 to 1.8 billion). The population of all less developed regions would increase by 60 percent, from 4.9 billion to 7.8 billion (with a low-to-high-variant
range of 6.4 billion to 9.3 billion). Meanwhile, the population of
industrial countries, the slowest-growing countries in the world,
would decline slightly, by 3 percent between 2000 and 2050, from
1.19 billion to 1.16 billion (low-to-high variant range from 990
million to 1.36 billion). For the year 2000, the best estimate is a
world population of 6.06 billion, with about 1.19 billion, or 20
percent, living in regions classified as more-developed. As of the
early 1990s the annual population growth rate of the "least-
developed countries"—mostly though not entirely in Africa—
was 2.5 percent, that of all less developed countries 1.8 percent,
and the more-developed countries 0.4 percent.

During the early 1990s, the "more-developed" industrial
countries—most notably Japan, Germany, Italy, Spain, France,
the Scandinavian countries, Russia, and most of the countries of
eastern Europe and the Baltic states—experienced an average
annual "total fertility rate" of 1.7 children per woman, well

below the level known to demographers as "replacement" (the level at which a hypothetical generation of women would replace themselves with a new generation of women of reproductive age, typically 2.1 children per woman in such countries).

In any such discussion, it is important to describe the many limitations afflicting these concepts of "total fertility rate" (TFR) and its conventional "replacement" rate of 2.1 for low-mortality settings. The total fertility rate is a "period" rate, in that it is designed to measure fertility during a specified year or other time period. The total fertility rate is defined as the average number of live births that a woman would have if she were to bear children through her reproductive lifetime at the rates observed for women of different ages during a specified year or other time period. So defined, it is a hypothetical or synthetic rate, in that no actual group of women experiences the rates summarized by the TFR, but it has the advantage of reflecting current fertility rates. The fertility of actual women is best measured by a "cohort" rate such as the completed fertility rate, which presents the average number of children produced by an actual cohort of women by the end of their reproductive years (normally defined as age 50). While a cohort rate has the advantage of measuring fertility of actual women, it reflects mainly the fertility experiences of these women during the preceding two to three decades.

The total fertility rate measure is attractive because it relates to recent fertility behavior, but many users are unaware of its deficiencies. Most notably, a population in which the age at marriage and/or childbearing is on the rise will produce annual total fertility rates that are substantially distorted below the true level of fertility, that is, the cohort rates that actual generations of women will average by the end of their childbearing years. One recent analysis develops adjustments for this "timing" or "tempo" distortion of the total fertility rate, and shows that the reported below-replacement fertility in the United States during the 1970s and 1980s was due largely to an increase in the age at childbearing, and that properly adjusted fertility rates during this period were essentially constant at close to two children per woman. For Taiwan, similar adjustments increased the estimated total fertility rate from well below the replacement level to very close to it: from around 1.7 to 2.0 in the period 1985–1993 (Bongaarts and Feeney 1998: 286).

Such distortions almost certainly afflict the total fertility rates calculated for other countries (for example, in Europe) in which the age of childbearing has been rising, but such effects have been difficult to quantify due to the absence of data on true birth order for women (whether married or not); instead the data deal with birth order within marriage, which makes adjustment for tempo effects impossible (Bongaarts and Feeney 1998: 286). A second analysis (Lesthaeghe and Willems 1999) accepts the conclusion that period total fertility rates ("period TFR") in Europe are distorted downward by ongoing increases in the age of childbearing, but speculates that even when such distortions disappear, currently very low fertility rates will remain well below replacement level.

Fertility is the main factor determining the age composition of most populations. High fertility rates produce youthful age composition; low fertility rates the opposite. Hence, while the proportion of the population of developing countries is young compared with that of industrial countries—and in some cases growing younger—that of populations of industrial countries aged 65 and over is large and increasing.

Thus the two major demographic consequences of the differential population growth rates of developed and developing countries are (1) a gradual shift in the distribution of the world's population from developed to developing countries and (2) population aging in low-fertility societies and the persistence of youth bulges in high-fertility societies.

One obvious question, then, is whether demographically slow-growing societies are also likely to be economically slow-growing, while the demographically dynamic societies are likely to grow faster economically by virtue of their expanding markets. There is, however, no clear relationship between population growth and economic growth. There are countries with all possible combinations of these two growth rates: high population/high economic growth; high population/low economic growth; low population/high economic growth; and low population/low economic growth. While per capita incomes are obviously shaped by the relationship between population and economic growth rates, a complex set of factors affects a country's economic growth rates, of which demographic factors are one, but by no means among the most important.

The relationship between national military power and population size and growth is also too complex to reduce to a simple formula. Countries with large economies and large populations clearly have a greater potential for military power than countries with smaller economies and smaller populations. Large economies—India, China, Indonesia—have the resources for military development that smaller economies with equally low per capita incomes cannot manage. These countries can more readily invest in nuclear weapons, delivery systems, and satellite communications, and, other things being equal, can create larger armies than can countries with smaller gross domestic products. From a strategic viewpoint, population size matters.

The willingness to employ force may also be influenced by demographic considerations. It has been argued that countries with rapid population growth have been more willing to send their sons to fight than countries with lower rates of population growth. It has certainly been the case that governments with conscript armies have sought to shield families with only one (surviving) son—the story of the 1998 film *Saving Private Ryan*. But here too, a simple relationship between demographics and state military strategies is not apparent. The reluctance of NATO countries to deploy their military forces in the Balkans or in Iraq cannot be reduced to demographic explanations. Nor can one attribute the high-risk military policies pursued by the Saddam Hussein regime to a willingness to expend lives in a demographically growing society, without factoring in the lack of accountability of an autocratic regime.

Looking toward the future, much is decidedly hazy. Efforts to predict long-term population trends have not been particularly successful, nor have efforts to predict which countries will be the economic powerhouses of the future. Estimates of future population growth made by well known demographers in the 1930s, when fertility rates were declining throughout Europe, reveal how difficult the task is. In 1936 the Royal Institute of International Affairs published a study (Carr-Saunders, 1936) which assembled the estimates of Europe's leading demographers. The demographers predicted that the population of Great Britain (45 million in 1933) would stabilize at 32.7 million by 1976. In fact Britain's population continued to grow, reaching 57.4 million by 1990. The estimates were similarly off for France. Demographers anticipated that the population (41 million in 1935) would level at 39 million by 1980, but by 1990 the population of France was 56.4 million. The estimates were also badly wrong for Italy, projected to increase from 42 million in 1933 to a peak of 60.6 million by 1961. In fact, Italy's population growth rate declined more rapidly than projected, so that Italy's population in 1990 was only 52.7 million.

Fertility rates can be affected by economic conditions, changing opportunities for women, tax policies, public policies toward child care, housing costs, inflation rates, and changing cultural norms. Moreover, even current low fertility rates in the United States and in many European countries may result from decisions of many women to temporarily defer having children. For these reasons, long-term estimates of the population of the Western world in relation to Asia and Africa should be regarded with caution. Having said that, there is little doubt that there has been a major demographic shift away from the Western world during the past century which seems likely to continue. In a sense, this represents a reversal of the major demographic shift toward the Western world that took place during the eighteenth and nineteenth centuries.

There have also been major demographic shifts among the developing countries, with the population of Africa increasing by more than threefold between 1950 and 1995—significantly higher growth rates than those experienced by Asia and South America, and well above the historic population growth rates of Europe, North America, and the former Soviet Union.

Migration is another central component of demographic projections, and yet it is even more difficult to forecast than fertility. As the relationship between population size and national power is problematic, so too is the relationship between population growth and migration. Historically, high-population-growth countries have experienced high rates of emigration, though there is no evidence that the growth rates closely correlated with emigration rates. Economic demographers have noted—contrary to conventional wisdom—that countries experiencing high rates of economic growth have also been major population-exporting countries (see, for example, Easterlin 1961 and Hatton and Williamson 1994). Note the high emigration rates from Europe in the nineteenth century, the period of Europe's greatest economic growth, and, for that matter, the continued emigration in the 1980s and early 1990s from the high-economic-growth countries of East Asia to Southeast Asia and to the United States. There are also regions that have experienced very high population growth rates—Java, for example, and Bangladesh—that have not produced large numbers of emigrants. All these counter-intuitive examples remind us of how little we still know about the determinants of large-scale population movements.

Estimates of future international migration flows are less reliable than estimates of natural population increases, since these are largely determined by government policies. Migration to Germany, for example, was as high as 300,000 for some years, near zero for others. Migration to the United States, Canada, and Australia, the three major migration countries, fluctuates substantially year-to-year. Annual migration to the United States was under 300,000 in the early 1960s, but rose to 700,000 per year in the 1980s and higher still in the 1990s. There have also been very substantial annual flows of labor migration to the Middle East, but these too fluctuate annually, shaped in part by the price of oil as well as by political conditions in the region.

Refugee flows constitute still another uncertain variable. A renewal of warfare in the former Yugoslavia, or new outbreaks of violence in Africa, could lead to significant population shifts. A study prepared by the Population Reference Bureau (Lutz 1994) estimated annual international migration flows at approximately 4.4 million, or about 4 to 5 percent of the annual increases in the world's population, a small number and percentage from a global perspective though larger for some regions of the world. Hence from a global perspective international migration is a minor factor in population growth as compared to the influence of natural increase; it is particularly minor in moderating rapid population growth for countries of emigration. It is, however, far more significant at a regional, national, and subnational level, as we shall see.

The uncertainty of these global demographic trends makes it all the more necessary to be cautious about predicting how changes in the distribution of the world's population might affect the security of states. More fundamentally, it is not clear that population size—except when it has a significant bearing on a country's gross domestic product—tells us much about national military power. Small countries with well-developed high-tech centers can develop weapons of mass destruction—chemical, biological, or nuclear—and if they have a high gross domestic product they can spend money on importing costly military technologies, including delivery systems. Technology has leveled the playing field, making demographics less important than in the eras of mass conscript armies, though not irrelevant. Poor countries with low economic growth rates and high population growth rates are clearly vulnerable to internal turmoil and are likely to be producers of refugees, while countries with low rates of population growth and high rates of economic growth may (or may not) be receptive to an influx of migrant workers.

If historical experience rather than formal demographic projections from the present is our guide, we would be well advised to expect the unexpected, anticipate the unpredictable, as a substantial influx and outflow takes place in some regions and among some countries, driven less by demographics than by political circumstances.

Note

1. For a fuller discussion, see chapter 3.

— *Two* —

POLITICAL DEMOGRAPHY
A Deficit of Attention

—◈◈◈—

In a study prepared for the National Academy of Sciences in 1971, one of the authors (MW) coined the concept of "political demography" to analyze the political consequences of population change. The concept was defined as follows:

> Political demography is the study of the size, composition, and distribution of population in relation to both government and politics. It is concerned with the political consequences of population change, especially the effects of population change on the demands made upon governments, on the performance of governments, on the distribution of political power within states, and on the distribution of national power among states. It also considers the political determinants of population change, especially the political causes of the movement of people, the relationship of various population configurations to the structure and functions of government, and public policies directed at affecting the size, composition, and distribution of populations. Finally, in the study of political demography it is not enough to know the facts and figures of population—that is fertility, mortality, and migration rates; it is also necessary to consider the knowledge and attitudes that people and their governments have toward population issues. (Weiner 1971: 567)

Although the concept may have been new in 1971, the issues raised by political demography had long antecedents in political and social theory, going back to the writings of Plato, Aristotle, and later Jefferson, on the relationship of population size and the establishment of constitutional government and stable authority. In addition to these classical concerns that stretch back into antiquity, three other broad areas were noted. One was the concern by European scholars in the 1930s with the impending decline of Europe's population and its impact on economic growth and on generational conflict over the distribution of government resources. A second was the concern by American scholars in the 1960s with the potential impact of rapid population growth in developing countries on political instability, violence, aggressive behavior, communism, revolution, and intense nationalism. And the third was a literature by scholars of international relations on the impact of population growth on international conflict as the result of aggressive behavior by countries feeling "population pressures."

The National Academy of Science study argued for the development of a new empirically based field of political demography, and suggested five areas of future inquiry involving various types of population changes and their potential political consequences: (1) an examination of the political and policy consequences of changes in the age structure of a population, notably a rise in the young age group in developing countries and a rise in the older population in developed countries; (2) change in family size and its impact on housing and on the fragmentation of land holdings, especially in developing countries; (3) the political effects of changes in population size and density on central/local relations and regional income disparities; (4) differential population growth rates among ethnic and religious communities and their effects on social and political relations, on the politics of the census, and on political representation; and (5) the political consequences of migration both within and across borders.

A final section of the study noted that the growth of population affected the kinds of demands made upon governments, raised issues of government management, and had an impact on how governments thought about military manpower. It suggested that population policy was more likely to be linked to issues of race, tribe, caste, and religion than to questions of class, and that the probability of political conflicts arose when the youth cohort grew more rapidly than the expansion of opportunities for employment. It also raised questions about how changes in fertility and mortality rates might affect child labor and women in the labor force. The study concluded with a call upon political scientists to develop a new field of political demography.

In the three decades since the essay was written, surprisingly few political scientists have addressed these issues. One reason is perhaps that the relationship between demography and politics seemed so elusive. For every conceivable relationship, one had to point to intervening variables. The impact of an expanding number of young people on political violence and revolution, for example, seemed to have more to do with the transition to a modern industrial economy or to large-scale unemployment than with numbers alone. Population pressure on resources and on the environment often depended on the character and rate of economic growth. Moreover, the greatest threat to global security came from the Soviet Union and its allies, where demographic variables played a negligible role.[1] By themselves, demographic factors appeared to explain very little of what interested political scientists.

A second reason is that the field of demography is seen by political scientists as largely atheoretical. To most with interests in social and political theories, demography is a dry subject with an arcane focus on the measurement of population size, composition, and territorial distribution and detailed studies of fertility, mortality, and territorial movement. Many social scientists are largely ignorant of demographic theory and methods, and look upon demographers as engaged in technical and dull work, data-gathering and number-crunching. The only major theory in the discipline of demography was the concept of the "demographic transition," long since revised if not rejected, while the most well-known founding father of the discipline, Thomas Malthus, had been repudiated by all but a handful of demographers. Many political scientists saw little in the way of theory or methods that could be borrowed from demography.

What political scientists unwisely neglected, however, others studied. Ecologists, some of whom were neo-Malthusians, were concerned with the race between population and resources, notwithstanding a decline in the price of many of the world's resources. Economists and demographers looked with considerable sophistication at the complex relationships between population growth and development. Biologists were interested in the earth's carrying capacity. Environmentalists worried about the deteriorating effects of population growth on local and global environments, while others emphasized the role of affluence.

The one field of political demography in which political scientists have made significant contributions has been in the study of migration, both within and across international boundaries. Here the security dimensions are particularly pronounced, since large-scale international population movements can both affect and be affected by the cohesion of societies and social and political conflict within and between countries. We shall turn to this subject in due course.

While political demography attends to both the political determinants and political consequences of population change, obviously it is the latter—the political consequences—that is most relevant to this volume. Given that our focus is on political consequences, and more narrowly upon implications for political and economic security, what matters is not only the empirical facts underlying demographic trends, but in addition the ways in which such trends are perceived by political elites and publics. In short, in terms of politics and security, both reality and perception matter.

While such issues may have been little addressed by contemporary political science, they have attracted the attention of some of the leading theorists of politics and society, from ancient times to the present.[2] The idea that there is an "optimum population" most suited to political order and economic well-being can be found in the writings of ancient China, of Plato and Aristotle, and of the greatest of the medieval Islamic historians, Ibn Khaldun. Later political theorists, including prominently Thomas Jefferson, saw close connections between the nature of civic life and politics and the levels of demographic densities in agrarian versus urban settings.

Economic writers, too, paid a high level of attention to demography as central to economic well-being and political stability. The mercantilists, who dominated European political and economic thought during the sixteenth and seventeenth centuries, saw a growing population as a means to increase the power and wealth of the absolutist monarch, and to this end advocated monarchical controls and interventions to increase fertility and restrain emigration. The free-market physiocrats who challenged them saw land resources rather than population as the principal source of wealth, and rejected government controls as counterproductive. Utopian thinkers of the eighteenth century believed that any population size would be sustainable so long as resources were equitably distributed. They in turn were challenged by classical economists led by Adam Smith and John Ricardo, who foresaw decreasing agricultural returns to labor and capital inputs, advocated free markets rather than state controls, and argued that such a free-market regime would regulate population increase in an automatic manner. Malthus went further by arguing that population growth left unrestrained would impoverish the lower classes, and instead urged voluntary restraint by means of delayed marriage and celibacy outside of marriage. (It is fascinating to note that, contrary to conventional modern understanding of his views, Malthus actually was opposed to the use of interventions such as contraception and abortion, which he considered to be "unnatural" and "vice." It was the so-called "neo-Malthusians," active decades after his death, who advocated voluntary contraception, although they too opposed abortion.)[3]

In opposition to the arguments of the classical economists and Malthusians, conventional Marxist-Leninist writers of the nineteenth and twentieth centuries argued that any level of population could be sustained under socialism, which would ensure (paralleling the earlier arguments of the utopians) that wealth and income would be equitably distributed. Ultimately, such traditional Marxist-Leninist views were subjected to challenge during the 1980s and 1990s, especially in the People's Republic of China. After much debate, Chinese Communist leaders concluded to the contrary, that unrestrained population increase presented a profound threat to the future of socialism. They promulgated strong state interventions in support of both Malthusian (marriage) and neo-Malthusian (fertility) restraint, the latter to be implemented via both contraception and abortion.

During these same two decades, political commentators associated with the American New Right embraced the earlier arguments put forward by utopians, mercantilists, and traditional Marxist-Leninists that population trends were not problematic if the correct economic system were in place. They rejected Malthus's attribution of poverty to excessive population growth, arguing instead that "economic statism" was the cause of poverty, and that population size would be self-regulating under a free-market system.

Impacts on Security

Although the question has not been addressed by most political scientists, it is important to consider the extent to which the size, density, and rate of increase of populations can be shown to represent important factors affecting security, both external and internal. The evidence available is decidedly mixed.

If we consider first the questions of raw military power, there would be little argument that—other things being equal—governments of populous states have more of the resources needed for such power than do those of small states. The "other things being equal" qualification is important here, since among the ten most populous countries in 1998, only two (the United States and Japan) would be considered prosperous developed countries. (The others are, in order of population size: China, India, Indonesia, Brazil, Pakistan, the Russian Federation, Bangladesh, and Nigeria [United Nations 1999: 3, Table 2].) However, it is still the case that by virtue of sheer size, the governments of all of these countries can command larger national budgets than would be available if they had the same per capita income but smaller populations. Moreover, many of these countries (especially China, India, Brazil, Pakistan, and the Russian Federation) have significant numbers of highly sophisticated scientists and engineers; if their governments wish to devote significant fractions of their national budgets to the development of nuclear weapons, missiles, and other technologies of war, they can do so in a way that countries with small populations and low per capita incomes cannot. (Of course, small countries with high per capita incomes can also succeed in such technologies on their own, or can form alliances with others for joint developments of this type.)

The relative importance of population size versus economic and technological resources is difficult to assess. Suffice it to say that the case of Israel demonstrates that even a state with a tiny population base is capable of creating its own homegrown high-tech defense capabilities that can make it at least the equal of far more populous neighboring states.

To what extent might one argue that countries with large populations tend to be more aggressive toward their neighbors? Certainly arguments about the needs of large-population countries to control additional territory was central to the *lebensraum* rationales used by German and Japanese expansionists during the 1930s.[4] Echoes of such arguments as they relate to less-developed countries can be found in a 1965 article by the eminent American demographer Philip Hauser:

> [T]he larger of these nations are not apt to remain hungry and frustrated without noting the relatively sparsely settled areas in their vicinity. The nations in the Southeast Asian peninsula … even parts of thinly settled Africa may be subject to the aggressive action of the

larger and hungrier nations as feelings of population pressure mount. (Hauser 1965: 65–66)

Yet the truth is that while most of the countries with large populations possess more or less potent military forces, they show no consistent pattern in their propensity toward exercising their military power in an aggressive manner.

The same skepticism seems in order about claims that countries with higher population densities tend to be more aggressive toward their neighbors. Although the concept of population density sounds straightforward, a simple ratio between numbers of people and the amount of land or housing stock within a country are inadequate conceptions for studying the frequency and kinds of interpersonal contacts in a society. Measured in this way, overall density may be low, but because there is little arable land the population may be highly concentrated. Or density on the land may be increasing, while density per room is declining with an increase in housing stock. Population in the center of large cities may be declining if people move to outlying districts, while density in modes of transport, and hence perceived crowding and congestion at peak travel times, may be rising rapidly. In short, there are different densities at work, at home, in transportation, and even different densities at different times.

Finally, what about the rate of population increase? Do countries with rapid demographic growth exhibit tendencies toward aggressiveness or political instability? The question arises frequently, yet the evidence is quite inconclusive. (For further discussion, see chapter 4.)

Most commentators, especially those writing before the twentieth century, focused on the political consequences of three aspects of population: size, density, and rate of increase. While these may indeed be important, there are other demographic elements embodying political consequences relevant to security concerns. These include changes in age structure and changes in ethnic composition.

Change in Age Structure

The age structure of a population is of critical interest to demographers, but has been less than well understood in many other fields. Age structure can, in principle, be affected by all three of the elements of demographic change: fertility, mortality, and migration. Of these, the first is quantitatively the most important. A country with a high fertility rate will have a youthful age composition, while one with low fertility will have an older age structure. It follows that a population in transition from high to low fertility will experience a shift in its age structure from more to less youthful—colloquially known as "population aging." Similarly, a shift from lower to higher fertility will cause a population's age structure to become more youthful. (There is no obvious English antonym for "aging" that could be used to describe this phenomenon.)

A decline in mortality can also affect age structures, but in more complex and countervailing ways. Reductions in infant and child mortality tend to produce a shift toward higher proportions of children and youth, while reduction of mortality among the elderly tends in the opposite direction. Under normal circumstances of mortality decline, from initially high levels death rates decline among all age groups, although typically more rapidly among the young. After overall mortality rates have declined to low levels, further declines may be differentially concentrated among the older age groups. The result is that mortality declines *per se* have no uniform impact on age structure, either across countries or over time, and the overall magnitudes of such effects tend to be modest relative to the effects of fertility changes.

Finally, migration can affect age structures, given that migrants (at least those of the economic type) tend to be concentrated among certain age groups—typically, young adults. Yet because such age groups are also at the peak of their childbearing years, such migrations also tend to include a heavy concentration of young children, and in some cases the elderly parent generation as well. Hence the effects of migration on age structure are, like those of mortality change, less concentrated in their impacts on age structure than are fertility changes.

The Youth Bulge Hypothesis

Consider the case of a country with high fertility rates (and therefore a youthful age composition) that also experiences a rapid decline in mortality from previously high levels. Empirically, such a mortality decline results from dramatic declines in infant and child mortality, thereby increasing even further the concentration of young persons in the population. In fact, this has been the experience of many developing countries in the period since World War II, resulting in the appearance of an exceptionally large youth cohort. In many modern developing countries, half the population is below the age of 25; sometimes half is below age 20. Such "youthful" age structures purportedly help to explain the growth of Islamic fundamentalism from Algeria to Afghanistan, marauding bands of adolescent armed warriors in sub-Saharan Africa, youth protest movements in Teheran (1970s), Manila and Seoul (1980s), and Jakarta (1990s), and the large-scale flight of young people across international borders in search of jobs or safety. Even in industrialized countries, far smaller concentrations in the "youth" age groups are said to explain the rise in drug-related crimes in U.S. and European cities, and youth protest movements in France and the United States (1960s). Of all the hypotheses concerning the relationship between demography and security, this proposition is surely among the most widely believed.

The youth bulge hypothesis—overdrawn as it may appear—resonates with a widely held and probably correct view that single men from ages 15 (or younger) to 25 can be dangerous to social order if they are not employed, disciplined by educational institutions or by the military, or under parental or community control.[5] The youth bulge hypothesis thus postulates a relationship between social controls and the size of the youth cohort: If the rise in the number of young men is accompanied by a diminution in social controls, the level of youth protest and violence is likely to increase. Moreover, social controls are likely to weaken when there is a rapid increase in the size of the youth cohort. There probably is a biological basis for assuming that young men (but not young women) are potential threats to social order, but that need not concern us here. At the least, the youth bulge proposition meets the media's sound-bite test: Wherever and whenever the media report there are mass demonstrations, terrorism, secessionist movements, clashes among ethnic groups, riots, and pogroms, one finds a disproportionate number of young men.

There are three related but distinct youth bulge hypotheses. Each postulates a relationship between an increase in the number of young people and one or more political consequences.

The first is that an increase in the number of young people in a society results in a change in demands upon the state. With a rise in the number of infants, there is an increased demand for health services. A growth in the 5 to 15 age group is likely to lead to an increased demand for more primary and secondary schools and for the training of more teachers. A rise in the number of college-age youths means that more institutions of higher learning may need to be built, or older ones enlarged. With an increase in new entrants into the labor force, there is a rise in the demand for employment. Family formation also puts pressure on the housing stock. If the private sector does not respond to these demands voters may call upon the state for increased investment in medical care, schools, colleges, and housing. Other demands for public services may follow—from the provision of drinking water to the disposal of urban waste. As the number of school-age children increases, educational planners are confronted with a moving target. Substantial increases in government expenditures are needed simply to keep the same proportion of children of school age in schools. Increased private and public private investments are also needed to keep up with the annual entrants into the labor force.

The second hypothesis is that a youth bulge will, as already suggested, lead to the rise of political protest movements, most especially if there are limited opportunities for employment. What do young men do if they are not employed? In the seventeenth and eighteenth centuries, prior to the introduction of compulsory military service in Europe, many young men of violent disposition joined local mercenary forces. When central authority erodes and radical movements develop, young unemployed men may be recruited by warlords, private armies, and paramilitary organizations. Throughout contemporary Africa young men are the backbone of mercenary forces in the service of political freebooters whose goals are to acquire control over the state's resources, especially the production and sale of oil, minerals, and drugs. Armed young men in the service of warlords engage in looting for themselves and their families.

Expansionist states can send their young abroad, to fight, administer, or colonize. Service in the colonies has been an honorable and profitable activity, one which also protected the state against the claims of its own citizens. In the absence of external outlets for the young, including opportunities in the colonies, there is a high probably of an internal implosion, with young men turning their aggressive behavior inward toward local authorities.

In the latter part of the eighteenth century, it is estimated that 40 percent of the French population was between the ages of 20 and 40 and only 24 percent was over 40 years age. When economic hardships prevailed between 1785 and 1794, unemployed young people formed an explosive population group, contributing to the revolutionary unrest within France and to the military ventures of the Revolutionary and Napoleonic wars.

By the latter part of the nineteenth and early part of the twentieth centuries, the proportion of young people was declining in Western Europe, but their number was increasing in Eastern Europe, the Balkans, and in Russia. One might plausibly argue that the various nationalist and revolutionary upheavals that beset Europe from the late eighteenth through the twentieth centuries coincided with the various youth bulges—in France at the time of the Revolution, in Germany and elsewhere in central Europe in the nineteenth century, then in Eastern Europe, in Russia, in the early part of the twentieth century. Yet such an argument clearly would overdetermine the role that demographic forces played and underestimate the impact of a host of other determinants.

Over the past several decades, a growing percentage of Third World populations have been young men, many of whom possess arms. In Iraq arms have been used not only against the country's neighbors but by the state against its own citizens. Elsewhere arms have been used by localized warrior groups to conduct internal wars—for example, in Afghanistan, Angola, Mozambique, Somalia, Sudan, Rwanda, Burundi, Zaire, Sierra Leone, and Liberia. The two most unstable regions of the world—the arc of Muslim-populated countries from Morocco to Afghanistan, and the countries of sub-Saharan Africa—have the highest population growth rates and large cohorts of young men readily recruited into political activist movements (in Muslim countries) or into local armed militias (in Africa). The annual rates of population growth in these two regions is near or above 3 percent, with population-doubling times of less than a quarter of a century. Even if fertility rates decline, population growth rates in both regions will continue to be high for succeeding decades, given the young age structure of these countries, through what demographers call demographic momentum.

Matthew Connelly and Paul Kennedy (1994: 34) write that a major threat to security is "demographically driven social unrest, political instability and regional wars," an elusive potpourri of determinants. Mass protests by young people have surely contributed to bringing down governments. Youth protest demonstrations in Tokyo, Seoul, Paris, Chicago, Berkeley, and Beijing did not overthrow governments, but they played a role in Jakarta, Manila, and Teheran, and they were decisive elements in separating Bangladesh from Pakistan. "Taking to the streets," writes Adam Gopnik (1998) "rarely seems to be an expression of the popular will, but is always a test of how much will is left in power." Still, a government that regards itself as having legitimacy, that has confidence in itself, is in command of the police and the army, and is willing to exercise force, can break up youth demonstrations. Youth protest movements test the will and capacity of authority, but do not necessarily bring it to its knees.

A third hypothesis is that a youth bulge leads to an increase in emigration. Throughout the nineteenth century, the era when the youth bulge took place in one European country after another, there was virtually no limit on worldwide migration for Europeans willing to settle in the colonies in Africa and Asia, in North and South America, and in Australia. For the United States, there were also opportunities for internal colonization with the availability of free land in the western territories. The mass migration from Europe in the nineteenth century accompanied the largest period of economic growth and technological innovation that any region of the world had ever experienced. Less clear is whether any or at least how much of the emigration was related to demographic factors in the receiving countries; what one can say with greater certainty is that the migration from Europe westward stimulated economic growth in the then sparsely populated receiving countries, which in turn served to attract additional migrants.

Changes in Internal Demographic Composition by Region, Ethnicity, Race

In addition to changes in the composition of a population by age, demographic trends and differentials can alter population composition by other characteristics that typically are deemed important in cultural or political terms. If, for example, the population of a given region grows more rapidly than that of another, the balance of national political power may shift over time toward the former region. If a socially defined category such as an ethnic or national or racial or religious group experiences faster or slower demographic increase than other such groups, its relative influence may similarly wax or wane over time.

As a general rule, such shifts are slow and incremental, and can be accommodated by the normal processes of gradual adjustment. They can, however, become problematic in political or security terms when they are unusually rapid or are driven by forces seen as unlawful or illegitimate (such as illegal immigration from other countries). In recent years, there have been all too many high-profile episodes of bloody ethnic strife that seem to be driven in part by competitive fears resulting from such compositional shifts. These include the several civil wars in the former Yugoslavia; violent confrontations in the northeastern states of India; and the turmoils and genocides of the Great Lakes region of Africa, including Rwanda, Burundi, and the former Zaire. In the following chapter, we turn to a more detailed discussion of these and other forms of demographic competition and their consequences.

Notes

Portions of this chapter are drawn from Weiner (1971).

1. For an opposite viewpoint, see Wattenberg (1987).
2. See Weiner (1971); Teitelbaum (1988, 1992, 2001).
3. For a fuller discussion of this perhaps surprising fact, see Teitelbaum (1988).
4. For a discussion of the Japanese arguments, see Rager (1941).
5. Car insurance rates are typically highest for this same age-sex group, offering an example of a quite different kind of such an age-bulge that is based on actuarial evidence.

— *Three* —

DEMOGRAPHY AS COMPETITION?

Demographic competition between states, ethnic groups, and many other categories of human society is a time-honored phenomenon. Before the rise of liberal democracies, such competition typically took military and economic forms, in which the monarch sought to maximize his or her power and wealth by increasing the size of the population as a source of both warriors and labor. Later, as the notion of political franchise and democratic elections spread, the size of subgroups in a population became an important factor in determining the political power and influence of politicians claiming to represent them.

So long as military prowess was determined by the size of one's army rather than its training and technology, it was evident that population size was of strategic significance, and a major factor determining national and imperial power. Innovations such as the military use of horses and steel swords allowed rulers controlling smaller populations to dominate larger ones (see, for example, Diamond 1997), but in general it was to the advantage of ambitious leaders to control larger populations as a source of military manpower.

From the sixteenth through the eighteenth centuries, the intellectually dominant mercantilists saw both military and economic advantage to larger populations. "One should never fear there being too many subjects or too many citizens," wrote Jean Bodin in 1576, "seeing that there is no wealth nor strength but in men." Nearly two centuries later, the size of the ruled population was still seen as constituting the essential wealth of the sovereign. "[T]he number of the people," said Frederick the Great, "makes the wealth of states."[1] This view, along with the mercantilists' commitments to the monarchical system, led them to urge state interventions to encourage fertility and discourage emigration.

The weight of elite opinion began to shift late in the eighteenth century, with the rise to prominence of the physiocrats in France and the classical economists in England. The physiocrats saw land resources as wealth and rejected the monarchical absolutism of the mercantilists. Classical economists such as Smith, Ricardo, and Malthus saw land as a fixed resource and anticipated decreasing agriculture returns to inputs of both labor and capital; they warned that increasing population size might lead to poverty rather than wealth.

Many decades later, with the crushing defeats of the Franco-Prussian War in mind, French intellectuals and political leaders began to shift again, back toward the arguments of the mercantilists that population size determined the military power and economic wealth of the state (although in nineteenth-century France this was applied both to the republican and the monarchical state). One of the most prolific intellectuals addressing the subject at that time was Paul Leroy-Beaulieu, professor in the College de France and the editor of *L'Economiste français*. In his 1881 journal, he wrote the following lugubrious pronouncement about the strategic implications of France's relatively slow demographic increase:

> It takes courage to tell the truth to one's country and to destroy those illusions that will bring us new reverses and new catastrophes. In the presence of a Germany of 45 million inhabitants and who will be 60 million in 20 years and 80 million in 50 years, and who can count on the loyalty of the Austrian populations, all the hopes of armed revenge are chimeras, sentimental and patriotic illusions, singularly dangerous for our country. (Teitelbaum and Winter 1985: 19)

Leroy-Beaulieu's advice was for France to redirect her efforts to build national power in the direction of overseas empire, instead of suicidal attempts to retake Alsace and Lorraine from the Germans. In particular, he urged French annexation of Tunisia as an appropriate first step.

Such strategic concerns spread widely among the French intellectual and political elite. Arsene Dumont, a demographer with very different (anticlerical Republican) views from those of the conservative Leroy-Beaulieu, nonetheless embraced his strategic view from a Republican perspective, by arguing in 1890 that "a nation must have a population dense enough to keep stable an equilibrium with her neighbors. [Otherwise France would be] at the mercy of monarchical and reactionary Europe" (Teitelbaum and Winter 1985: 20). British commentators agreed, with one noting explicitly in 1902 that because of its slow demographic growth, "France's old desire for revenge upon Germany has now probably lost much of its strength" (Teitelbaum and Winter 1985:20).

As early as the late 1890s, an organization entitled the National Alliance for the Growth of the French Population had been founded in Paris; among its founding members was the novelist Emile Zola. In the decades prior to World War I, concerns about impending armed conflict heightened apprehensions about the connections between demography and military power. In 1909, Alfred de Foville, President of the Academie des Sciences Morales et Politiques, wrote as follows of the dangers facing France, dependent as it was on an army of conscription:

> Militarily speaking, we have an increase in feebleness which accounts for the growing scantiness of our annual conscription, while abundant reinforcements grow in the armies in contrast to which, we have been unable to keep pace since 1870. That being so, what can our sons and grandsons hope for in future conflicts, regardless of how valiant they may be?"(Teitelbaum and Winter 1985: 20–21)

Such concerns, although certainly exaggerated, were based upon demographic realities that were hard to ignore. In 1906, some 1.2 million men were mobilized in Germany, of whom over 500,000 were aged 20 and 670,000 had been deferred in earlier years. In that same year, France could mobilize only 368,000–318,000 aged 20, and 40,000 previously deferred. With this three-fold numerical advantage, the German army needed to induct only 26 percent of the original pool into the regular army; the rest were sent home to support their families, or placed in a series of reserve categories (Teitelbaum and Winter 1985: 21–22). Around 1910, the German male population in the peak military age groups of 20–29 numbered over 5 million, nearly 75 percent larger than the comparable groups in France at about 3 million (Mitchell 1980: 46–47; Teitelbaum and Winter 1985: 23, Table 2.1).

Notwithstanding such concerns, in World War I demographically dynamic Germany lost the war of attrition on the Western Front. Yet the demographic anxieties of the prewar period persisted. In fact, during the 1919 French parliamentary debate on ratification of the Treaty of Versailles itself, the French Premier Georges Clemenceau gave the following analysis:

> The treaty does not say that France must undertake to have children, but it is the first thing which ought to have been put in it. For if France turns her back on large families, one can put all the clauses one wants in a treaty, one can take all the guns of Germany, one can do whatever one likes, France will be lost because there will be no more Frenchmen. (*Journal officiel* 1919, quoted in Teitelbaum and Winter 1985: 36)

Only five years later, Premier Poincaré pointed to the "military problems" produced by low fertility (Teitelbaum and Winter 1985: 37). The French decisions of the 1930s to retreat behind its Maginot line and to accelerate rearmament with the mechanized tools of war were seen as the only means by which a demographically stagnant France could hope to compete with Germany. In the words of Paul Reynaud, a prominent minister in the 1930s government led by Deladier and a leading proponent of mechanized rearmament, "there is only one factor that dominates all: the demographic factor" (Teitelbaum and Winter 1985: 37).

Other French leaders, while in agreement with the diagnosis, proposed other treatments. One was to call upon France's by then substantial empire: "[W]e can take from our marvelous colonial domain the troops needed to match Hitler and his 67 million Germans," said one (*Journal officiel* 1937, quoted in Teitelbaum and Winter 1985: 37). Others called for measures to increase the French birth rate, as if unaware that any additional births would not be of military service age for another 15 to 20 years.

The Great Depression of the 1930s was also a factor raising concerns about low fertility. Although most visible among French commentators, they were shared by many others, including the Swedish Nobelist economist Gunnar Myrdal, who worried that low fertility rates were depressing economic demand, investment, and hence economic growth:

To my mind no other factor—not even that of peace or war—is so tremendously fatal for the long-term destinies of democracies as the factor of population. Democracy, not only as a political form but with all its content of civic ideals and human life, must either solve this problem or perish. (Myrdal 1940: 22)

In this he echoed earlier writings by the leading British economists, Hobson and Keynes. Hobson, who had served as a member of the unofficial National Birth-Rate Commission, which met intermittently between 1913 and 1926 under the auspices of the National League of Life, was reported by its leader Reverend James Marchant to have said that low population growth rates were perfectly compatible with his theories of underconsumption (Marchant 1920).

Keynes too argued during the 1930s that a higher birth rate would increase the marginal propensity to consume, and this in concert with multiplier effects would increase the rate of investment and economic growth (Keynes 1937).

Lest anyone incorrectly conclude that these representations are only from the past, consider the following comment from a 1984 interview in the left-wing newspaper *Liberation* by Jacques Chirac, at that time Mayor of Paris and later elected to the French Presidency:

Two dangers stalk French society: social democratization and a demographic slump.... If you look at Europe and then at other continents, the comparison is terrifying. In demographic terms, Europe is vanishing. Twenty years or so from now, our countries will be empty, and no matter what our technological strength, we shall be incapable of putting it to use. (as quoted in Teitelbaum and Winter 1985: 123)

Concerns such as these have been most visible in French political discourse, but have by no means been limited to the political class in Paris. During the 1930s, such concerns were widely expressed in industrialized countries experiencing very low period fertility rates. Germany under the Nazis, and the Soviet Union under Stalin, both undertook concerted policy initiatives intended to raise fertility rates for explicitly strategic reasons.

Australia and Canada, both former British colonies with huge but sparsely populated land masses, were also countries that for decades pursued a policy of population expansion with a strategic intent. At the time of Federation in 1901, the "white Australia policy" was uniformly supported across the political spectrum.

Population policies were "built on fear, firstly in an attempt to keep the 'yellow races' out and secondly to build up the numbers of Anglo-Celtic sons of Empire in defence of the young nation" (Cocks 1996: 2). William ("Billy") Hughes, Australian Prime Minister during World War I, popularized a slogan in this genre— "Populate or Perish"—as a way to emphasize how important it was for the Australian population to increase to a size sufficient to secure its territory from the possible depredations of far more densely populated neighbors in Asia.

During World War II, this perspective was invoked as the basis of Australia's now-traditional policy of encouraging immigration:

> The greatest single need for future development and national greatness, argued the influential men of Australia, was more Australians. In December 1943, when Australia's population numbered 7 million, Prime Minister Curtin told the nation that only a population of 20 million could guarantee Australian security; several months later he increased the number to 30 million. Politicians of both parties adopted William Hughes' old slogan: "Populate or Perish." Because natural increase alone could never suffice to populate the country in accordance with the ambitions of the country's leaders, they called for massive immigration. In 1946, the Minister for Immigration, Arthur Calwell, arranged with the British government to provide free passages to Britons who wanted to migrate. When the numbers proved insufficient, Calwell and his successors made similar agreements with the governments of Holland, Italy, Greece, Yugoslavia and other European countries. Subsequently, Australia's post-war population grew at a rate of 2 percent per annum, a doubling every 35 years, a growth rate similar to those obtaining in undeveloped countries. In 1955 Australia received the one millionth post-war immigrant. Between 1947 and 1980 Australia gained nearly three million new settlers, representing over 58 percent of post-war population growth. (Lines 1992: 199)

In one sense this policy represented continuity from the past. As World War II ended, Australians of widely differing perspectives were

> well aware that as an isolated European enclave occupying a huge land mass (which most believed could support a far larger population than the 7.5 million then present), they needed more (preferably British) people. These beliefs had been the basis for previous systematic attempts to bring British immigrants to Australia, programs that had continued throughout the nineteenth and twentieth centuries except during periods of war or depression.... The Second

World War and the narrow escape from Japanese invasion had brought these concerns to the forefront of the postwar political agenda. (Birrell and Birrell 1981: 44)

Mysteriously enough, for much of the twentieth century politicians in Canada also proclaimed that it would be highly desirable to see the population of that country grow to 30 million. The origins of this Canadian target number are uncertain, but it has taken on a mythic character and is rarely if ever challenged.[2] It may perhaps represent a downward adjustment of an implausible forecast propounded much earlier in the century: In 1904, Prime Minister Wilfred Laurier enthusiastically predicted that there would be 60 million Canadians—a ten-fold increase—within the lifetimes of those in his audience (Gooderham 1995).

In 1984 the Canadian government convened an expert group to consider the fertility decline that had occurred in Canada during the preceding decade. The group described continuing population increase as "one of the major factors contributing toward a dynamic society." The experts called for costly financial incentives to raise fertility, justified by comparing them with defense expenditures and asking "whether the goal of maintaining the population was not as important as that of national defence. Perhaps as much could be spent for the first as for the second; in the long term, there is no point in 'defending' a population that is disappearing!" (Government of Canada 1984).

Such strategic concerns have always been defensive rather than expansionary, but they may be driven by worries about possible expansionary tendencies of neighboring countries with higher population densities and more rapid rates of demographic increase. Unsurprisingly, this is more true in cases where there has been a history of controversy concerning borders and sovereignty. The fractious eighteenth- and nineteenth-century disputes between the United States and what is now Canada have not been forgotten in Canada; nor have Australian commentators forgotten the real threats that were posed by Japanese military expansion during the 1930s and 1940s, justified in part by Japan's alleged need for more land for its large and rapidly growing population. The similar *lebensraum* justification for German military invasions in the 1930s and 1940s has also not been forgotten in Europe, although few would express concern about a Germany that now has some of the lowest demographic growth rates in the world, and has proven itself to be a stable liberal democracy with close ties to its neighbors both politically and economically. (For more discussion of *lebensraum*-type arguments, see chapter 4.)

In the United States such concerns have been more muted. However, as recently as 1987 one visible American political journalist based much of an entire book (Wattenberg 1987) and many of his syndicated columns on the claim that the West "is committing slow-motion demographic suicide." His principal argument was that higher fertility in countries of the "industrial Communist world" would lead to their ascendancy over the West by 2085. He bolstered his assertions with robust-appearing 100-year demographic projections which he attributed to a "Special World Bank Projection." In fact, the only thing about the book's projections that involved the World Bank was that Mr. Wattenberg's research associate persuaded a World Bank demographer, My T. Vu, to run Mr. Wattenberg's own assumptions about future fertility, mortality, and migration through the World Bank's projection software. Since all projection outputs depend solely upon their input assumptions, the projections appearing in Wattenberg's book could hardly be fairly described as a World Bank product.[3]

Moreover, as noted at the time by one expert on Soviet demography, the USSR fertility and mortality rates Wattenberg chose— and then held constant for 100 years—were quite dubious, even for the early 1980s: His chosen fertility rates were higher than the apparent levels at the time, and his mortality assumptions ignored evidence that mortality conditions were deteriorating.

A review of Wattenberg's book by one of the present authors, published in the 1987 *Congressional Record*, comments: "One wonders ... what political scientists would make of forecasts that hold national characters and military alliances constant for a full century; put another way, if Wattenberg had been writing 100 years ago, when the Czar ruled Russia and Britain ruled the waves, what would he have predicted about the relative strength of NATO and the Warsaw Pact in 1987?" (Teitelbaum 1987).

Within only a few years of the publication of what Wattenberg himself described as "this alarmist tract" (Wattenberg 1987 [1989]: 10), the Warsaw Pact, and eventually the Soviet Union itself, dissolved into political and economic chaos. Anyone taking the time to read this book now in light of subsequent events can see that the arguments it put forth so recently and with such enthusiasm were embarrassingly defective. Yet it is sobering to note that Wattenberg's claims seem to have been convincing to political leaders of considerable stature, such as Senator Daniel Patrick Moynihan and Ambassador Jeane J. Kirkpatrick (Wattenberg 1987: back cover), apparently innocent of the perils of taking dubious long-range demographic projections to be forecasts.

The Population Senescence Hypothesis[4]

The youth bulge hypothesis discussed in chapter 2 above, has its analogue at the opposite extreme of the age distribution. In this formulation, populations with "old" age compositions (typically resulting, as the reader will recall, from low levels of fertility) are afflicted by a kind of "demographic senescence"—a lack of political vigor, creativity and ambition, economic vitality, social dynamism, and military prowess. Lest anyone doubt the force of such concerns, consider the following comment written in 1946 by Robert Debré (father of Michel Debré, later to become the first premier of the Fifth Republic) and the eminent French demographer Alfred Sauvy:

> The terrible failure of 1940, more moral than material, must be linked in part to this dangerous sclerosis. We saw all too often, during the occupation, old men leaning wearily towards the servile solution, at the time that the young were taking part in the national impulse towards independence and liberty. This crucial effect of our senility, is it not a grave warning? (Debré and Sauvy 1946: 58)

In another setting, Sauvy characterized an aging society in memorable terms, as one made up of "old people, living in old houses, ruminating about old ideas" (Teitelbaum 1978). Again, in 1981, Sauvy explained the nineteenth-century decline of French naval power in terms of its demographic aging: "The decline of the French Navy was more severe than in other countries. Under the influence of population aging, the French Government and Parliament subsidized the Navy's sailing ships while other countries were adopting steam-powered craft" (Sauvy 1981: 234).

While such concerns were particularly strong among the French political class and intellectuals, they were shared by other prominent European scholars and statesmen. Gunnar Myrdal expressed concern that an older age structure would make it harder for younger people to advance in their careers, and thereby reduce society's impetus toward progress:

When on account of the changed age structure individual opportunities to rise socially are blocked, people will get discouraged. They will lose their dynamic interest in working life. Society will lose the mental attitude that goes with progress. Interest in security will be substituted for an earlier interest in social advancement. (Myrdal 1940 [1962]: 165)

Demography as Internal Competition[5]

Within virtually all societies, some groups increase their numbers more rapidly than others. Fertility rates and mortality rates (especially for infants) often vary markedly from one socioeconomic class to another, from one ethnic group to another, and from one geographic region to another. Some social groups may be augmented by immigration, while others may not. If sustained over extended time periods, such differences can produce substantial shifts in relative numbers. And to the extent that numbers constitute an element in the political power of social groups, we can say that differential rates of population growth affect the distribution of political power within a society.

How important is the size of a social group as a determinant of its political power? We do not wish to suggest any precision in assessing the importance of raw numbers, given the importance of other variables such as the cohesiveness and organizability of a social group, the skills of its leadership, its financial resources, or its ability to provide or deny needed goods and services to others. Moreover, the "mix" of such variables depends heavily upon the kind of political system in which the group operates—whether it is democratic or not, the kind of system of political representation it has, or how important elections are in the political system.

For our purpose it is sufficient to note first that the size of a particular social group, and particularly of an observable ethnic group, is a factor in its political power, particularly in democratic systems. And second, in many political systems, different ethnic, socioeconomic, and geographical groups often *perceive* differences in their relative size and growth rates as factors affecting the distribution of power. A few examples should suffice to demonstrate how differing population growth rates—or perceptions of such—can affect the distribution of power within political systems and affect the relationships among social groups.

The Former Soviet Union

Some of the largest fertility differentials among regional and ethnic groups in the same country were seen in the former Soviet Union. Throughout the seven decades of the Soviet regime, differentials that were already visible in the Czarist Empire persisted. Broadly speaking, the Soviet regions of the west and north emulated the fertility trends in the other industrialized countries of Europe, while fertility rates in the Central Asian republics resembled those of south Asia. By 1980/81, fertility (as measured by the period total fertility rate) for the Russian Federation and for the Ukraine had reached 1.9, while those for Tadzhikistan, Turkmenistan, and Uzbekistan were reported to be 5.6, 4.9, and 4.8 respectively (Jones and Grupp 1987: Table 2.11). A decade later, on the eve of the breakup of the USSR, the range had narrowed, but not by very much. Fertility averaged 2.3 for the whole of the USSR: still 1.9 in the Russian Federation and in the Ukraine, but 5.1 in Tadzhikistan, 4.2 in Turkmenistan, and 4.1 in Uzbekistan (Haub 1994: 13 and Table A-3).

Data on changes in the ethnic composition in the Soviet Union are difficult to interpret.[6] While there appear to have been major declines, for example, in the percentage of the population reported as Ukrainian during the period 1926–1939 (from 21.2 to 16.5 percent of the Soviet population over this 13-year period), this shift was probably attributable in great measure to changing official definitions of ethnic status that led to persons previously classified as Ukrainians changing to "Russians," along with differentially high mortality in the region due to the forced collectivization and famine of the early 1930s. Hence these data should not be over-interpreted: The dominant finding from the Soviet Revolution to around 1960 is that the relative size of the major cultural groupings of the USSR—Slavs, other Europeans, and Muslims—showed relative stability. Over the period 1920–1959, the dominant Slav group declined only from 78.0 percent in 1926 to 77.1 percent in 1959; the sharp decline in the Ukrainian percentage was balanced by a substantial increase in the percentage reporting Russian nationality.

After 1960, this relative stability rapidly disappeared. In the two decades from 1959 to 1979, the percentage represented by the dominant Slav group declined from 77.1 percent to 72.8 percent, while the Muslim percentage increased sharply, from 11.5 to 16.7 percent. This shift resulted from the very high fertility rates among the Muslim populations, coupled with rapid declines in their rates of mortality. Average annual rates of demographic increase among Uzbeks, Tadzhiks, and Turkomans approached 4 percent during the 1960s—rates rarely seen in human populations other than those in the Arab Middle East and Kenya.

Such exceptionally high rates of population growth naturally attracted the attention of analysts both within and outside the Soviet Union. During the 1970s and early 1980s, Soviet writers tended to avoid commentary on the high fertility rates of the Central Asian Republics, emphasizing instead the low fertility of the Slavic populations. Elsewhere, there was speculation about the implications if such differentials were to continue—would the long politically dominant Russians become a minority of the Soviet population (Feshbach 1979: 656–709; Meyer 1978; Wallace 1977)? Although Muslim fertility began to decline during the 1970s, the Muslim population nonetheless reached 20 percent by 1990—substantially lower than had been projected by some assuming continuation of the very high 1960s fertility rates, but still understood to be a rapid rate of ethnic change.

However, until toward the end of the 1980s, the subject was one of great political delicacy, and was treated as such. At that point, however, the debate became more unrestrained. Slavic ethnic alarm became more open, more strident—in many ways similar to that expressed in nineteenth-century France (Szporluk 1989; Hajda and Bussinger 1993).[7] In the French case, the issues involved attracted the energetic attention of Emile Zola; in Russia in 1990, none other than Alexander Solzhenitsyn published an essay replete with the gloomiest of demographic forecasts, entitled "Rebuilding Russia": "Everyone knows," he wrote from exile, "our mortality grows and surpasses the births, and thus we shall disappear from the earth."[8]

Earlier, in 1986, *Moskva* magazine had published an article by an exiled Russian economist, Mikhail Bernstam, entitled "How Long Will the Russian People Live?"[9] Bernstam's essay deploys the extraordinarily long-range projections that are common in such writings, and concludes that if then-present trends were to continue, there would be only 23 million Russians left by the year 2200. It is a perhaps an ironic accident of timing that in the same year that Bernstam's essay appeared in English translation,

Wattenberg used his own long-range projections to argue almost precisely the opposite: that should fertility in the West remain low for a century, the Warsaw Pact would rise to political and economic supremacy.

Russian commentaries on Bernstam's article indicate a lack of awareness that the low Russian fertility levels causing such concerns were very similar to those of other industrialized countries. Consider, for example, this excerpt from the editors' foreword to the *Moskva* article:

> Of problems inherited by us from the epoch of stagnation, the most serious is the demographic crisis of the European populations of the USSR, the Russians in the first place, the people who, to tell the truth, has in fact commenced to die out. It has got the lowest fertility potential in the world, and if the present-day trends continue already in the next century all Russians, i.e. East Slavonic peoples—Russians, Ukrainians, Byelorussians—will cease to be a major world population group and become a small insignificant ethnic group scattered in the territory which will be settled by other peoples....
>
> Bernstam's forecasts may plunge one into despair. He has forecast ethnic death, a fast demographic catastrophe.... But despair is the lot of the weak.... The Russians were on the brink of a national, including demographic, catastrophe not [only] once.... But every time it resurrected, its number grew. The Russian people possesses specific metaphysical properties not grasped by rational thinking, which permitted it to honorably get out of the most difficult situations. The scale of the threat menacing it increase[s] tenfold its strength, energy and vitality. (*Moskva* 1986)[10]

By the late 1980s, the battle over ethnic fertility differentials had been joined in open fashion. The Turkmenian demographer Sh. Khadyrov was quoted as follows:

> In the first half of the 1980s, a whole group of demographers supported the thesis about the necessity to do away with the demographic exclusiveness (that is high fertility) of whole peoples with the help of widespread propaganda and proliferation of modern contraceptive methods and active involvement of women in economic activity.... The situation that should be feared most and which was prophesied by Western Sovietologists thus emerged. The latter were saying that the Kremlin, at some time or other, would be forced to pursue two demographic policies: one aimed at increasing the fertility in the European part, where families with a small number of children are prevalent, and [the] other aimed at its reduction in Central Asia.

There is no better means of provoking the tension between ethnic groups. (Vishnevsky 1993: 7)

With the dissolution of the USSR in 1991, such internal debates about differential fertility generally disappeared. But in the economic instability that ensued, fertility within the Russian Federation declined and mortality (especially of adult males) increased. The total fertility rate reportedly declined from 2.2 in 1987 to 1.6 in 1992, and 1.3 in 1993. During 1993 alone, male life expectancy declined by 3.6 years to 59 years, and female by 2 years to 72; the gap between male and female life expectancy reached the unprecedented peacetime level of 13 years.

Demographic alarums continued to be sounded. A Commission on Safeguarding the Health of the Population, established by the Security Council of the Russian Federation, concluded in July 1994, "A demographic catastrophe in Russia is no longer a potential possibility, it is a *fait accompli*"(Baiduzhy 1994). The trends "aroused fears among nationalists who lament that it will soon begin to affect Russia's status as a great power"(Cienski 1994). In September 1994, Vladimir Zhirinovsky, leader of the ultra-nationalist Liberal Democratic Party of Russia (LDPR) was reported in the Western press to have announced that "the catastrophic demographic situation creates a direct threat to the Russian nation." According to these reports, he announced that he would respond with a very personal crusade: Zhirinovsky gave orders "to ensure that at least one child by the chairman of the LDPR personally be born in each regional branch of the LDPR in 1995," for which purpose the party would make "appropriate monetary allocations" from its budget (Washington *Post* 1994b).

In addition to fertility differentials, the presence or absence of migration can also powerfully affect the rates of growth and decline of particular ethnic and regional groups. Like all states, the USSR exercised control over entry by non-nationals, but it was distinctive in also controlling both the international departure and the internal migration of its own citizens. Most Soviet citizens were not allowed to travel abroad, but exceptions were made during some periods for a few ethnic and/or nationality groups with external homelands (Jews, Armenians), often in response to international pressure. As a result of these exceptions, the proportionate share of the USSR population accounted for by these groups tended toward decline.

As to Russians themselves, there was some migration to other countries during the 1920s by those opposed to the Bolshevik Revolution, but in the ensuing five decades from the 1930s to the 1980s there was remarkably little emigration. There was, however, very substantial Russian migration from Russia to the "near-abroad," the non-Russian Republics of the USSR, especially after World War II. The Soviet government encouraged these Russian migrations on economic grounds, especially regarding skilled personnel needed for industrialization. But it seems likely that migration by Russians to these peripheral regions also was encouraged to strengthen Slavic influence upon non-Slavic or non-Russian republics such as Azerbaijan and the Baltics. By the late 1980s, as the USSR moved toward dissolution, some 25 million Russians were resident in non-Russian republics (Brubaker 1993: 49). Such a large internal migration somewhat reduced the numbers of Russians within Russia, but also clearly changed the ethnic distributions of the non-Russian republics, in some cases quite dramatically. For example, at the time of independence, Estonia's population was fully 30 percent Russian, and that of Ukraine 22 percent.

Although these Russian migrants had never moved across national boundaries, most were later to find themselves residents of newly independent sovereign states. In some (but not all) cases, these people were viewed as a threat by the indigenous non-Russian population, and subjected to a variety of forms of discrimination and mistreatment that caused the government of the Russian Federation to warn that it maintains a right to intervene to protect them from abusive treatment. During the 1990s, millions of Russians in the "near abroad" migrated back to the Russian Federation, again shifting the ethnic balance in Russia and in the former Soviet republics.

Ireland

Another example of current interest may be found in Ireland. In this case, a political problem faced by the nineteenth-century hegemon (Britain) was moderated by both a shift in the proportions of the United Kingdom population who were Irish, and the proportions of the population in Ireland who were Catholic and Protestant. Overall, the Irish population (including Northern Ireland) actually declined by one-third from the middle of the nineteenth century to the middle of the twentieth, from 6.8 million to

4.6 million. The causes of this dramatic population decline are well known: the desperate famines that cruelly increased mortality and lowered fertility, coupled with massive emigration to the United States, Canada, Australia, and elsewhere. This decline in the Irish population occurred as the population of Great Britain was increasing from 21 million to 50 million, thereby greatly reducing the proportion of the total United Kingdom population represented by the Irish—from about one-third during the first third of the nineteenth century to only one-seventh by the 1880s. As a result, the relative significance of the Irish population in the UK lessened, and

> [t]his made a vast difference in how the United Kingdom was willing to cope with the Irish problem. One need only imagine how the British would have responded to the demand for independence if Ireland had been larger. The British would presumably have been even more fearful of an alliance between the Irish and the French and later between the Germans and the Irish. (Weiner 1971: 597)

Moreover, over this century-long period the population in Catholic regions of Ireland declined more rapidly than that in Protestant Ulster, thereby shifting the internal balance of the two main confessional groups on the island. Following World War II, however, fertility rates among Irish Protestants declined more rapidly than did those of Irish Catholics. As a result, over the ensuing decades the proportions of children and then young adults who were Catholic increased, and especially so in Northern Ireland. This was also a period during which Irish nationalism (largely Catholic) and concerns about discrimination against Catholics in the North rose to the fore. Though there may not be a causal connection between these trends, they did converge in time.

Canada

Much of Canadian history has focused upon the linguistic divide between Francophone Quebec and the other mostly English-speaking provinces and territories. In the eighteenth century, Quebec fertility rates were nearly the highest of recorded human experience; more recently, Quebec fertility is close to the lowest in the world. This change, coupled with high rates of immigration of non-francophones, has produced substantial internal demographic change, and much in the way of heated political debate.

Overall, Canadian fertility rates declined by some 40 percent during the 1960s, from a postwar baby boom level of about 3.9 children per woman in 1960 to 2.3 in 1970, paralleling a similar rapid decline in the neighboring United States. During the 1980s and early 1990s, the decline continued, reaching 1.64 in 1995 (*M2 Presswire* 1997). In Quebec, the decline was even more dramatic. The eminent French demographer Louis Henry had immortalized the eighteenth-century Québecois as demonstrating the second-highest fertility levels ever recorded—second only to the Hutterites, an Anabaptist sect whose religious commitments favored exceptionally high fertility (Henry 1961). By the 1980s, Quebec fertility rates were among the lowest in the world, along with those of West Germany, Italy, and Hong Kong, while fertility rates in the rest of Canada remained much higher. By the mid-1990s, however, the fertility gap between Quebec and the rest of Canada had closed: Quebec fertility increased from 1.37 to 1.61 children per woman between 1986 and 1994, while fertility in the rest of Canada declined (*Financial Post* 1994; *M2 Presswire* 1996).

As fertility rates in Quebec declined rapidly during the 1960s and 1970s, continuing high rates of immigration became more important demographically, and immigrant children whose mother tongues were neither French nor English (known in Canada as "allophones") were showing a strong tendency to become anglophone. These trends evoked considerable anguish among Quebec nationalists as to the long-term future of the province's French-speaking population. Their concerns may have been exaggerated, but they were not entirely unfounded: Demographic projections of 50 years ago showed the Quebec population exceeding that of Ontario by the 1970s, yet by 1995 the Quebec population was only 65 percent of Ontario's (*M2 Presswire* 1996).

Late in the 1960s, founding leaders of the Quebec separatist movement began to write with alarm about these demographic trends. The late René Levesque (founder of the separatist Parti Québecois in 1968, and Premier of Quebec from 1976 to 1985) wrote:

> French Quebec itself is, literally, in danger of death. Several factors ... emphasize the deterioration of our relative population strength. First of all the birth rate has decreased at a dizzying rate.... Emigration, for its part, acts against us.... Finally, there is immigration!
>
> From 1945 to 1967 inclusive, Canada accepted some three million immigrants. More than thirty-five percent, on the average, were of Anglo-Saxon origin. As for the French, there were 4,408 of them out

of 146,758 immigrants in 1965, or three per cent…. Nothing could be less surprising, for of thirty-five immigration offices six are in the United Kingdom and Ireland, five in Germany, and four in the United States….

We know the results of this policy for the rest of Canada. It has become a unilingual country where, in eight provinces at least, the French minorities are irreparably submerged.

As for Quebec, this policy combined with the falling birth rate is leading straight to a demographic catastrophe. (Levesque 1968: 92–93)

Included as an appendix in Levesque's book was an essay written in 1964 by Jacques Parizeau, who was later to succeed Levesque as leader of the Parti Québecois and Premier of Quebec until he stepped down in 1995. In this essay, Parizeau wrote:

In Quebec, it is now understood by an increasing number of people that the combination of a rapidly declining birth rate and the failure to assimilate immigrants into the French stream present dreadful dangers for the French community in North America. The reorganization of family allowances, facilities for working mothers, and new immigration policies became objectives of far greater significance than in the rest of Canada…. (Levesque 1968: Appendix 4)

Given such statements by its two founders and leaders, it was no surprise that after the Parti Québecois took power in the province in 1976, it adopted a variety of policy measures designed to raise Quebec's fertility rate, to gain provincial control over immigration to Quebec, and to require allophone immigrant children to be educated in French schools only. Notwithstanding the adoption of such measures and the increase in Quebec fertility rates from their mid-1980s lows, the tense Canadian political debates about language, sovereignty, and ethnicity can hardly be said to have been resolved. There have already been two referenda in Quebec on separation from the rest of Canada, with the second losing by 50.6 percent to 49.4 percent, and a further referendum promised by the Parti Québecois once the appropriate conditions exist. During his campaign for the latter sovereignty referendum, in 1985, Lucien Bouchard, then leader of the Quebec separatist bloc in the Canadian federal parliament and now Premier of Quebec, emphasized that "French-speaking Quebeckers have one of the lowest birthrates among 'the white races'" (Turner 1995: A10).

The United States

In the United States there were for decades very substantial differences between the fertility behavior of white Protestants and non-hispanic white Catholics, with the latter recording substantially higher rates. These differentials did evoke some expressions of concern from the former groups, and formed some small part of the rise of eugenics during the 1920s and 1930s. But by the 1960s U.S. Catholic fertility rates had declined to levels very close to those of Protestants, and such worries were no longer in evidence (Westoff and Jones 1979). Similar concerns were also heard in the United States about fertility differentials between whites and blacks, but these differences too have declined in magnitude and are no longer an issue appearing in public debate.

These examples point to a shift from concern with differential fertility rates among socioeconomic classes (an issue in much of Western Europe in the nineteenth century, when conflicts were mainly along class lines) to a concern with differential fertility rates among populations having different cultural values. Few writers in the United States would speak today as Gunnar Myrdal did as late in 1938 of "the great and obnoxious fertility differences between the overfertile poor strata and the underfertile middle and upper strata" (Myrdal 1940 [1962]: 22), but many comment on the changing proportions of racial, ethnic, religious, or tribal groups.

Yet differential fertility rates among such groups are of significance only insofar as the difference is seen as having a significant political effect. In the United States interest has waned in such differentials as fertility rates have tended toward convergence. Yet such differentials came to matter a great deal to political elites in settings such as Kosovo, Rwanda and Burundi, the former USSR, apartheid South Africa, and in various countries in the Middle East. In the latter region, for example, the government of Israel, the government of Saddam Hussein in Iraq, and Palestinian leaders in the West Bank, Gaza, and Jordan all have sought to encourage fertility in the interest of perceived national security and power.

The Role of Immigration

As may be seen in the contentious debates in Canada, substantial inflows of immigrants into a setting in which indigenous fertility is low can lead to rapid transformations of the population. This in turn may—or may not—produce contentious internal politics along long-established fissures of the society. Outcomes depend on a complex array of factors: the demographic distribution in the particular setting; the extent of fertility and mortality differentials among the indigenous population groups; the history of relations among these groups; the characteristics of the immigrants, including the extent to which they do or do not identify themselves with the majority or a minority group in the destination country; the extent to which the laws and practices of the destination country favor or disfavor the immigrant groups; and so on.

At the most general level, consider a population that has experienced low rates of demographic increase for many decades, such that its population size is constant. The entry of international migrants into such a population would then dominate its rate of demographic change. This would be an essentially meaningless statement, however, unless the numbers of such migrants are substantial (since the entry of a single migrant into such a setting would account for all of its demographic increase, but would be demographically trivial). If in fact the migrants' numbers are substantial and if they differ in ethnic terms from the indigenous population, then the ethnic composition of the destination setting could change very significantly. One obvious historical case would be that of the United States, where substantial immigration from Europe accompanied by increased mortality among the indigenous population shifted the territory's demographic composition from predominantly Native American to European within the course of less than a century. There is considerable evidence that the native population opposed this rapid demographic transformation, especially when European settlers began to compete for land. But they lacked the coercive and organizational capacities that would have been needed to turn the tide.

Similarly rapid internal demographic transformations are now possible in many settings in industrialized countries, especially those in which the fertility rates of some indigenous groups have declined to very low levels while others are considerably higher, or in which overall fertility rates are low but substantial inflows of immigrants are being experienced. The difference is that while efforts to increase fertility rates are generally rather unsuccessful, these societies do not lack for organizational and coercive capacity to affect migratory movements should they collectively so wish. Whether or not they seek to do so is essentially a question of politics, in which the interests of those who benefit from immigration (employers of immigrants; co-ethnics; political parties that hope to attract support; and so on) contest with those who believe they will lose (workers whose skill levels put them into competition with immigrants; ethnic/national/religious groups who fear loss of relative numbers, as when U.S. hispanic politicians announce that hispanics now outnumber African-Americans.

As might be imagined, such contentions can become deeply entangled with the otherwise technical questions surrounding the collection and tabulation of demographic data. In this regard, the politics of national censuses have become increasingly polemical over the past several decades, with passionate debates as to demographic categories such as "race" (Is "race" a legitimate category on which official data should be collected? How many "races" should be listed? Should individuals be able to indicate multiple races?) and "ancestry" (Which ancestries should be tabulated? How should multiple ancestries be classified?). In some national debates, for example that underway in France, some groups argue that it is morally intolerable for the state to collect data on national origin or race, whereas in other debates (as in the United States) these categories are viewed as increasingly important for purposes of allocating political power, employment, and public benefits. While "race" and "ancestry" are confusing enough, the issues are further clouded by the accretion in recent decades of crosscutting categories such as "hispanic" in the U.S. census (a "hispanic" may be of any race).

In some countries, the mere collection of national census data is so politically fraught as to have been avoided since the 1930s (Lebanon) or to have contributed powerfully to civil war and military takeovers (Nigeria).

The outcome of such debates is essentially indeterminate. It depends entirely upon a given country's particular configuration of political and interest-group forces; on its political structure (Can a political movement in this domain gain influence within the political system?); its geographical location and historical experience; and many other particularities that lead to the richness and diversity of political outcomes. Some groups may affirmatively renounce expressions of such concern (such as Protestant religious groups in the United States), whereas others may become more alarmed (Jewish nationalist groups in Israel). Coalition governments (such as those of Austria or Belgium or

Israel) may be more open to the concerns of such groups than are majority-party governments such as those that tend to rule in the United Kingdom or the United States.

While it is possible to offer some worthwhile analyses and commentary on the forces that underlie such crosscutting demographic trends and the politics they engender, it is almost impossible to provide credible predictions or forecasts of the outcomes that may emerge in a given setting.[11]

Notes

1. Frederick II (1712–1786), King of Prussia (1740–1786), was generally considered among the most notable of enlightened despots in eighteenth-century Europe. Frederick was most known for his successful policy of Prussian aggrandizement, gaining control of the duchies of Silesia, East Friesland, and much of Polish Prussia and Bavaria. He promoted new methods of agriculture and manufacturing, developed new lands for cultivation and colonization, and somewhat liberalized the institution of serfdom. The quotation is from Strangeland (1904).
2. Personal communication (MST), 1998, Robert Trempe, former Chair, Commission on Immigration, Government of Canada.
3. Personal communication (MST), My T. Vu, July 1987. For Wattenberg's description of the process, see *The Birth Dearth*, p. 169.
4. For a discussion in depth of such concerns, see Teitelbaum and Winter (1985).
5. This section is based in part upon Weiner (1971: 595 ff).
6. For a discussion of the difficulties involved, see Teitelbaum and Winter (1998: chap. 5).
7. For a detailed discussion of the French debate, see Teitelbaum and Winter (1985).
8. Solzhenitsyn's article was published in both *Literaturnaya Gazeta* and *Komsomolskaya Pravda*, in September 1990.
9. Translated in R. Conquest (1986). The original title of Bernstam's essay was "The Demograpy of Soviet Ethnic Groups in World Perspective."
10. *Moskva*, 1986, p. 4. Translated by A. Vishnevsky (1993), minor grammatical corrections added to translation.
11. For a book-length consideration of these and other related issues, see Teitelbaum and Winter (1998).

— Four —

DEMOGRAPHY AS AGGRESSION?

Larger populations need more resources, and hence people from societies with dense and/or rapidly growing populations tend to push outward, occupy territory, and exert pressure on other less demographically dynamic peoples. Islamic population growth is thus a major contributing factor to the conflicts along the borders of the Islamic world between Muslims and other peoples. Population pressure combined with economic stagnation promotes Muslim migration to Western and other non-Muslim societies, elevating immigration as an issue in those societies. The juxtaposition of a rapidly growing people of one culture and a slowly growing or stagnant people of another culture generates pressure for economic and/or political adjustment in both societies. (Huntington 1996)

The larger of these nations are not apt to remain hungry and frustrated without noting the relatively sparsely settled areas in their vicinity. The nations in the Southeast Asia peninsula: Burma, Thailand, and the newly formed free countries of Indo-China ... even parts of thinly settled Africa may be subject to the aggressive action of the larger and hungrier nations as feelings of population pressure mount. Moreover, Communist China, the largest nation in the world by far, faced with ... already heavy burdens ... may not confine her attention only to the smaller nations within her reach." (Hauser 1965: 65–66)

The richest soils were always most subject to changes of masters. The goodness of the land ... invited invasion.... Attica, from the poverty of its soil enjoying from a very remote period freedom from faction, never changes its inhabitants.... Victims of war or faction from the rest of Hellas took refuge with Athenians as a safe retreat; and become naturalized, swelled the already large population of the city to such a height that Attica became at last too small to hold them, and they had to send out colonies to Ionia. (Thucydides [1934]: 3–4)

From time immemorial, contemporary observers and historians have regarded demographic factors as a determinant of aggression, violence, territorial expansion, conquest, and colonization—in short, of all forms of behavior in which peoples or states expand their control over and at the expense of others. Demographic aggression is, therefore, by no means new, although which demographic variables are at work and what forms demographic aggression take vary in time and place.

We begin this analysis with a critical caveat. It is essential to distinguish between demography as explanation and demography as justification. Governments have often justified their aggression on demographic grounds—the classic example is the Nazi doctrine of *lebensraum*, the right asserted by Germany to expand and extend its territory in order to acquire greater living space for its people. Variants of this argument have been widely used by densely populated, rapidly growing countries to justify the extension of boundaries at the expense of weaker neighbors or to acquire colonial territories. When a notion of *lebensraum* becomes adopted as state doctrine, then it becomes both an explanation and a justification for aggressive behavior.

The view of some governing elites is that they lead a Great People who are morally and culturally superior to their neighbors, that they are ordained by history or religion to exercise control over others, and that they have the right to acquire the territory of other lesser peoples. Such views constitute a familiar self-justification for expansion. Johann Herder's theory of how modern nations were created out of folk cultures—the idea of a *Volk* (or people) subject to its own natural laws of development, the importance of language in this development, and the role played by literary intellectuals—formed the basis of modern nationalism in much of Europe, but said little about whether nationalism took a benign or aggressive form. Nationalism in its aggressive form promoted demographic expansion by providing a justification for the departure of populations to settle in others' territories. Thus can demography, embedded in political ideology, become the instrument of a form of aggressive nationalism.

There are four circumstances under which the concept of demographic aggression can be usefully applied.

The first presumes that within a given territory there is an imbalance between the demands of an expanding population and the limited capacity to meet these demands of the territory in which that population resides. The limiting capacity may be the territory itself, the land needed for agricultural production, its forests and water supply, and more broadly the technology employed by the resident population to use these resources efficiently. A nomadic hunting or gathering population, for example, will soon reach its limits if it does not change its food-gathering and agricultural practices when its population increases. The great historic movements of populations—from the Peloponnesus throughout the Mediterranean basin; from Rome to the empire in Asia Minor, Mesopotamia, and Africa; the Mongol invasion of Europe; the movement of Turks from Central Asia into Asia Minor; the movement of Slavs eastward from the Dnieper; the migration of Russians northward, southward, and eastward; and the vast movement of millions of Europeans to North and South America and Australia—were in part or in entirety driven by the search for land and opportunities for employment, although one should not underestimate the importance of security and military considerations in any of these migrations.

To call this form of demographic expansion "aggression" is, of course, to imply an intent that may not have been present, although from the point of view of the local population the migrations were often widely perceived as aggressive. That is surely the case with the movement of people of European origin across the American frontier occupied by Native Americans who regarded the migrants, armed and backed by U.S. militia, as an aggressive force. Similarly, central Asians fought against the Slavic settlements, and the people of northwestern India resisted the penetration of colonists and settlers from across the Hindu Kush. Whatever the motivations for migration, to the local population settlers often seem to be aggressors. This demand/capacity demographic model does not presume that either demand or capacity is fixed, but that the dynamic tension between the two is a source of conflict.

The second circumstance involves the use of international migration as a diplomatic or rhetorical tool. Some of the rhetoric of the new migration has been notably aggressive. President Mahatir of Malaysia, in a widely cited speech, spoke of the capacity of low-income countries to thrust their emigrants upon other countries unless there was greater equity in the distribution of the world's resources and unless, Mahatir argued, the West was prepared to provide new investments in the Third World.

A less intentional form of demographic aggression was described in vivid literary terms in a prize-winning French novel, *The Camp of the Saints*, written in the 1970s by Jean Raspail. Raspail describes in evocative terms the desperate journey of a flotilla of natives from India to the shores of France. In his apocalyptic vision, there were

> a million poor wretches, armed only with their weakness and their numbers, overwhelmed by misery, encumbered with starving brown and black children, ready to disembark on our soil, the vanguard of the multitudes pressing hard against every part of the tired and overfed West. I literally saw them, saw the major problem they present, a problem absolutely insoluble by our present moral standards. To let them in would destroy us. To reject them would destroy them. (Raspail 1995)

Raspail's novel received a great deal of attention in an article published in the *Atlantic Monthly* by Matthew Connelly and the eminent Yale historian Paul Kennedy (1994). The article, and the dystopic novel upon which it rested, came close to describing a demographic aggression model in which a desperate people can project power and influence through emigration toward liberal democracies.

"Discourse" matters, and if there is a growing view that emigration has become a weapon utilized by governments and ethnic groups to extend political, economic, or even cultural interests, then the level of conflict between migrants and residents could grow.

A third type of demographic aggression model draws from social psychological theories of crowding and density. This theory finds much favor in the popular media and among journalists, foreign affairs officials, and tourists to poor, densely populated developing countries with histories of violence: Haiti, Nigeria, Sri Lanka, Rwanda, Bangladesh, and so on.

Its argument draws on the commonplace that some threshold of population density is required for people to organize. Institutions that bring large numbers of people together provide one important condition for the creation of political organization: Factory workers are more readily organizable than peasants, and students in colleges and university are more easily organized than young people who are not in educational institutions. But while there may be a threshold of density below which people do not readily organize politically, is there another threshold of density above which people are more likely to be violent and aggressive? In a much-cited experimental study conducted in the 1960s, the social psychologist John Calhoun examined the effects of high density on the behavior of a domesticated albino strain of the Norway rat. As density increased, he reported, male rats became more engaged in struggles for status, fighting increased, mortality among infants and females increased, homosexuality among male rats grew, and some even became cannibalistic (Calhoun 1962: 13–146).

Notwithstanding such findings about rats, it remains quite unclear not only whether or not there is a higher incidence of pathological behavior among humans in densely populated than in dispersed areas, but also what constitutes pathology. Even so, one of the most universally believed social theories is the notion that those who live in rural areas and small towns are more likely to be virtuous, trustworthy, less violent, and more reasonable than those who are born and raised in high-density urban centers. Among Americans there has been a popular belief in the special qualities of public figures from small towns like Aberdeen, Kansas; Libertyville, Illinois; and Hope, Arkansas. The idea that where public figures spent their early years shapes their moral character is a widely shared belief in almost all societies, including and perhaps especially those societies that are densely populated.

As noted in chapter 1, population density is an elusive measure. What if one were to look instead at population growth rates, rather than density, as a possible factor in civil strife, violence, political radicalism? A list of the low-income countries with the highest population growth rates from 1960 to 1992 (those exceeding 3 percent annually) would include Costa Rica, Venezuela, Kuwait, Iran, Libya, Botswana, Saudi Arabia, Syria, Jordan, Paraguay, Oman, Iraq, Honduras, Zimbabwe, Pakistan, Kenya, Zambia, Comoros, Zaire, Côte d'Ivoire, Tanzania, Djibouti, Rwanda, Malawi, Uganda, Liberia, Gambia, and Niger. The population of each of these countries increased two-and-a-half fold during this period.

The low-income countries with the lowest annual population growth rates from 1960 to 1992, those that were 2 percent or lower, were Cuba, Argentina, Chile, Singapore, Jamaica, Sri Lanka, Lebanon, China, Haiti, Cambodia, Bhutan, Chad, the United Arab

Emirates, Fiji, Afghanistan, and Sierra Leone. If we include countries that grew somewhat faster, at 2.2 percent, but still below the high-growth countries, we would add Tunisia, Indonesia, Vietnam, Myanmar, India, the Central African Republic, Burundi, and Guinea.

It is hardly self-evident that the countries on the first list are more violent, have suffered more from ethnic strife and civil wars, have more youth-driven radical movements than the countries on the second list, or are demonstrably more aggressive states.

The fourth type of demographic aggression involves the removal of the indigenes, or "local" population. Removal can take place through forcible deportations by the state, threats to the safety and well-being of the local population through abuse by the state or by ethnic or economic groups antagonistic to the indigenes, or by a set of policies that benefit one group over another. The bottom line is whether the indigenes are in flight. Again, the question is often whether there is aggression—that is, whether reasonable observers would conclude that the indigene community legitimately feels threatened or discriminated against in some way and therefore has reason to be in flight.

There are countless examples of demographic situations in which one people has displaced another. Kulischer (1948: 8) noted that in A.D. 900 Berlin had no Germans, Moscow had no Russians, Budapest had no Hungarians, Madrid was a Moorish settlement, and Constantinople had few Turks. The Normans had not yet settled in Great Britain and before the sixteenth century there were no Europeans living in North or South America, Australia, New Zealand, or South Africa.

To Kulischer's 1948 observation one can add another list of more recent demographic transformations as a consequence of large-scale settlement and flight. At the beginning of the twentieth century Vilna was a Polish and Jewish city; by the 1940s it had been transformed into a Lithuanian settlement with no Jews and few Poles. Tel Aviv was Arab, the Greek city of Salonika had a large Turkish and Jewish population, the Turkish city of Izmir still had a large Greek population, the Chinese city of Urumchi (the provincial capital of Xinjiang) was Uighur, Danzig was German, the Ukrainian city of Lvov was Polish, and Sarajevo was a culturally mixed city, not Bosnian Muslim. The Black Sea region was colonized by the Greeks, who after centuries were no longer colonists but indigenes, whose culture had transformed Pontos. In the twentieth century Pontic Greeks and other Christian communities have been in flight from Turkish-Muslim rule, bringing an end to two millennia of a Christian presence.

The indigene population can feel threatened by settlers for a variety of reasons not limited to aggressive or clearly discriminatory actions by government. Hiring practices by the public or private sector, opportunities for admission into schools, colleges, and technical institutions, the right to use one's language in public life, are widely seen as indications of whether the state is discriminating against the indigene population; there may also be a "tipping" situation in which the indigenous community feels that the demographic situation has now shifted the balance toward the settler community.

Refugees and Displaced Persons

One of the most notable developments over the past quarter-century has been the worldwide increase in refugee flows and internally displaced persons. Might this suggest a connection between demography and levels of violence? There have been internal conflicts, including wars of secession by territorially based ethnic groups, wars by central or local governments against such groups (Eritreans, Kurds, Chechens, Southern Sudanese, Sri Lankan Tamils, Croats, Serbs, Bosnian Muslims), attacks against territorially dispersed ethnic groups (Tutsi and Hutu in Rwanda and Burundi), non-ethnic civil wars (Tadzhikistan, Mozambique, Angola, El Salvador, Nicaragua, Liberia, Algeria), and political persecution by authoritarian regimes (Iran, Iraq, China).

Internal conflicts rather than wars between states have been the principal generators of population flight in the post–Cold War era. Worldwide, the number of refugees has increased more rapidly than the number of countries producing refugees, from an average of 287,000 refugees per conflict in 1969 to 459,000 refugees in 1992. If the number of internally displaced persons is added to the totals, then the average number of refugees and displaced persons increased from 400,000 per conflict in 1969 to 857,000 in 1992 (Weiner 1996a). Seventeen of the thirty countries that produced large numbers of refugees ranked in the bottom fifth of the world's poorest countries. But is it the low level of development within these societies that explains the high level of conflict, or is it the high level of violent conflict that explains the low level of economic development?

An alternative explanation for the increase in refugee flows per conflict is that there has been a rise in the level of violence toward civilian noncombatants, the result of the easy flow of arms into the developing world and the ready use of antipersonnel mines. The widespread use of antipersonnel mines—an estimated 200 million worldwide—has had a particularly devastating impact on civilians and has generated massive flights from rural areas.

Several recent important social science inquiries into the determinants of ethnic violence place emphasis upon forms of civic life and social interactions among ethnic groups rather than upon demographic factors. Varshney, for example, argues that forms of engagement that bring communities together (or separate them) explain the presence or absence of ethnic and communal violence. He argues that a vigorous associational life which builds inter-communal ties constrains the polarizing strategies of political elites, who look upon communal conflict as a way of mobilizing political support (Varshney 2001, forthcoming).

* * * *

What can we conclude from the limited empirical evidence as to the relationship between demographic variables—population size, population density, or rates of population growth—and political violence, including aggressive behavior? There does not appear to be any clear empirical evidence to support the widely held view that low-income, high-population-growth, high-density countries are more violent or more likely to be aggressive than countries with higher per capita incomes, lower population growth rates, and lower population densities, or any combination of these variables.

While there is no clear answer to the question of whether or not demographic trends affect rates of violence, we can conclude that when violence does occur in countries with high population growth and density, there are more likely to be high mortality rates among children and large outflows of refugees and internally displaced persons than in countries that are less crowded and growing more slowly. At one level this proposition is banal: When there is violence, people who live in crowded places are more likely to kill or be killed than if the violence takes place in less crowded places. High-fertility societies have proportionately larger numbers of children, who are especially vulnerable under violent, disordered circumstances. From this perspective population density does not create violence, but it does explain the high mortality rates that result from violence.

At another level of analysis this is not a trivial observation, for it calls attention to the high level of vulnerability of large numbers of people who live in countries torn by violence, and to the problems faced by humanitarian organizations trying to provide protection for people at risk. Notwithstanding the many academic studies and the innumerable reports by national and international organizations, non-governmental organizations, and foundations purporting to explain violent conflict in developing countries, we still know very little about how to prevent violent conflict or how to halt it once it has begun.

What we do know is that violence in crowded places is highly destructive; if we are unable to attend to the violence, can we attend to the issue of crowding? To put the matter another way, are there ways of distributing or redistributing vulnerable populations so as to reduce their vulnerability? Does the concentration of large numbers of people in refugee camps operated by international organizations and NGOs put people at greater risk than if they were dispersed in smaller refugee camps or dispersed among local communities? Would refugees and internally displaced persons be at lower risk if they were provided protection in places farther from border areas or war zones, where arms and ammunition moved freely? Can alternative opportunities to combat be made available to young people—sports, employment, or income-generating activities—to reduce the chances that they would be recruited for armed conflict? Can effective international agreements be reached to prohibit the recruitment of child-warriors by governments and insurgents alike? How might better data on the demographics of conflict and on refugee flows be collected and how could they be better utilized to deal with vulnerable groups?

All of these questions deserve thoughtful attention, and some are being addressed by the United Nations High Commissioner for Refugees, by the United Nations Secretariat, and by a variety of non-governmental organizations concerned with containing violence among peoples already uprooted from their homes.

— Five —

DEMOGRAPHIC ENGINEERING
Settlement and Deportation

> The king shall populate the countryside by creating villages on virgin land or by revising abandoned village sites. Settlement can be effected either by shifting some of the population of his own country or by immigration of foreigners. The settlers in the villages shall mainly be Sudra agriculturalists, with a minimum of one hundred families and a maximum of five hundred. The villages shall be sited so as to provide mutual protection.
>
> Kautilya, *The Arthashastra*, 2.1.1.3: 179—fourth century B.C.

There are two ways to think about the relationship between demography and security. The first, addressed in chapters 1 to 4, is to consider how changes in demographic variables—in the size, distribution, and composition of a population—influence a country's political stability and its perception of threats to its security. The second is to examine how governments have sought to change demographic variables in order to enhance their security. We thus now reverse the causal arrows to ask these questions: Under what conditions do security concerns of governments lead them to attempt to affect—or "engineer"—demographic variables? What policy instruments do they employ? What are the security consequences for themselves and for others?

Demographic engineering entails the full range of government policies intended to affect the size, composition, distribution, and growth rate of a population. From this perspective demographic engineering includes the many policies pursued by governments to promote or slow population growth, including, for example, family subsidies to promote fertility and anti-abortion policies as well as pro-abortion policies. Many of these policies, it should be noted, have been adopted by states concerned about security, not simply development. As is well known, during the interwar period of the 1920s and 1930s both France and Germany promoted population growth as part of an effort to expand military manpower through conscription.

Forms of State Intervention

In our analysis of demographic engineering, we shall focus primarily on state policies to move or remove populations, for it is these interventions that have had and are likely to have significant effects on the security of states and of peoples. We consider five forms of state intervention.

The first is that of *addition*: policies to promote the movement of dominant national or ethnic groups as settlers into areas populated primarily by subordinate or minority groups. We use the term "settlers" here to denote people who have entered a territory under the auspices of political authority, distinguishing them from the more typical "migrants" who have moved without such encouragement.[1] Governments may engage in this form of demographic colonization through population transfers for any one or more of the following reasons: to establish the hegemony of a dominant ethnic group, to enhance their political control over a people or territory, to prevent the rise of secessionist or irredentist movements, and to diminish the prospects of arms flows and financial support to border populations.

The questions that need to be asked about the demographic strategy of addition are: Why are these migration settlement policies adopted? What policy instruments are employed to induce the migrations? What are the political responses of the local population to the settlers? Do the policies generate violent conflict and secessionist movements, or do they solidify political control? Do they lead to a refugee flight and conflicts with neighboring countries? In short, what are the internal and international security consequences of settlement policies?

The second is that of *subtraction*: policies designed to remove certain (often minority) populations out of the country or from one portion of the country to another in order to solidify national or regional identities or to enhance national security—in short, to "unmix" populations that may have lived mixed together over centuries. An analysis of policies to unmix populations by forcing flight would consider the circumstances under which such policies are adopted, the internal conflicts they generate, and their consequences for relations between the sending and receiving countries when the movements are across international borders.

Since forced population movements intended to unmix populations almost invariably provoke an international response, what are the options available to the international community for dealing with states that engage in such practices and in addressing the question of resettlement or repatriation of those who were forced to move?

A third demographic engineering approach, *substitution*, combines the first two by moving certain groups out while moving others in.

The fourth set of demographic engineering policies promotes *outmigration*—emigration to other countries so as to generate domestic and international benefits of both an economic and a political character. The governments of many migrant-origin countries either explicitly or implicitly follow this policy, in the belief that emigration provides a "safety valve" and thereby reduces political pressures among a domestic population which might otherwise become restive. They also expect to capture substantial economic benefits from the inflow of foreign exchange in the form of overseas-worker remittances to families remaining behind, financial investments from their overseas migrants, and increased inflow of technology from their higher-skilled nationals working abroad. Some seek further advantages of a political character, attempting to utilize their overseas populations to influence the domestic politics and foreign policies of the receiving country. In order to maximize such economic and political benefits, sending country governments sometimes invest heavily in efforts to sustain relations with their citizens who have migrated abroad. Some of the new transnational communities—people born in one country who live in another but retain strong cultural, economic, and political ties with their country of origin—have called for the establishment of dual citizenship, including voting rights, demands that pose awkward and increasingly contested issues of national identity and national security. Several countries have now granted dual citizenship or dual nationality to their overseas migrants. What are the likely consequences for the migrants, for their relationship with the local population, with their country of origin, and with their country of residence?

The fifth set of demographic engineering policies aims at *restriction of entry*. Control over entry is a core attribute of state sovereignty, and few question the right of governments to decide whom to admit for work, permanent residence, and citizenship. Globalization has diminished the importance of borders with respect to the flow of trade, capital, and information, but borders continue to be important in controlling the movement of people. The erosion of controls over the former, however, has made it increasingly difficult for governments to control the latter.

As illegal migration has grown and as government refugee and asylum policies have increasingly become used (and often misused) as vehicles for migration, governments have sought new ways to deal with unwanted entries. Many governments are using their military for control over land borders, not against invading armies but against illegal population entry, employing naval forces and coast guards to interdict ships with passengers seeking illegal entry or political asylum, negotiating arrangements with their neighbors to tighten their entry and exit points, and introducing tighter labor controls to deter employers of undocumented workers and to reduce the incentives for illegal entry. From a security perspective, important key questions are whether military forces can be efficacious in controlling entry, what kinds of military forces and techniques can be employed, whether their use jeopardizes trade and tourist flows across international borders, and what challenges they pose for the international refugee regime.

Settlement Policies

The movement of populations by governments as a strategy for establishing territorial control is an ancient practice. Conquest was a two-stage process: The first was military conquest, the second was colonization—the movement into a territory of one's own people to settle the land, build or gain control of the urban settlements, and establish the political authority of the victors. Examples abound: Greeks settled in Sicily, Romans and the Normans in the conquered Saxon territories; waves of invaders settled in northwestern India; the defeat of the Serbs by the Ottomans in 1389 was followed by the settlement of Muslims in Kosovo. With the purchase of the Louisiana Territory by President Jefferson, and the subsequent military victory over Mexico that resulted in the incorporation of much of the Southwest, the United States engaged in a systematic policy of land settlement. The movement westward—the so-called frontier policy—involved the extension of political control over newly purchased or conquered territories and the extension of political control over local populations—Native Americans or Mexicans. The real estate policies adopted by Congress provided the basis for land settlement by setting the terms of the use of "free" land, while military force was provided by the federal authorities to protect the settlements—on the whole, a policy very much in the spirit of Kautilya, quoted at the beginning of this chapter.

Turning to Europe and Asia, internal colonizations via population transfers have long been a widely employed demographic policy in both Russia and China. From the middle of the nineteenth century Russians moved to Central Asia, following the Great Game conquests of the Czars in Bhukara, Kiva, and regions to the north in what is now Khazhakstan. Under Stalin, Russians were induced to migrate to the newly conquered Baltic territories, and minorities (most notably Koreans) were removed from international border areas where they might seek arms and political support from their ethnic brethren. The process of Russification would later leave millions of Russian-speakers behind in the successor states to the Soviet Union, where their citizenship status has become problematic. Similarly, in Chinese Central Asia successive Chinese regimes pursued a policy of moving Han Chinese to areas under their control in Mongolia, Gunzu, Xinjiang, and Tibet. Since the Chinese government declared the annexation of Tibet in 1951, there has been a large influx of Han Chinese, in many cases encouraged by the Chinese government. Supporters of the Dalai Lama assert that this is a form of "cultural genocide," a planned effort to outnumber the few million Tibetan indigenes; in 1997 the Dalai Lama warned, "The very survival of Tibetans as a distinct people is under constant threat." In response, the Beijing government claims that the Han migration to Tibet is part of an ambitious effort at economic development for the desperately poor region. The Tibetan government-in-exile claims that Han Chinese already outnumber indigenous Tibetans; the Chinese government reports than less than 5 percent of the region's population are Han. Independent assessment of such claims is impossible, although one press summary estimates the Han population to be in the range of 15 to 23 percent of the total (Chu 1999).[2]

Although Russification and Sinification—the words imply both population colonization and the extension of the dominant culture and its language to native peoples—are perhaps the largest and most well known examples of internal population transfers, there are numerous other contemporary examples. These include the Philippine settlement of the Moros region in Mindanao; Javanese settlement of Sumatra and other outer islands; Burman settlement of the Bengali-speaking Rohingya areas near the borders of Bangladesh; Bangladeshi settlement of the Chittagong Hill Tracts with its Buddhist population; and Bhutanese settlement of southern Bhutan and the forced deportation of Nepali-speaking residents. Moving outside of Asia, there are the examples of Moroccan settlement of the disputed territories in the Western Sahara, and Israeli settlements in the Arab populated West Bank. South Africa under the apartheid regime instituted internal pass laws and systematically removed Zulu and other native peoples from white townships. Before World War II, the government of France encouraged French settlements in Algeria, an area they regarded as more than a colony but less than a French *département*. A similar policy guided the Japanese settlement policy of Manchuria in the 1930s and the Portuguese settlement of Goa, Mozambique, and Angola.

What were the consequences? Did colonization solidify political control by the state over its territories? In some instances, the answer is clearly yes. By sheer numbers, political control, and military action, the United States settled the territories to the west, leaving the Native American and Mexican populations in subordinate economic, social, and political conditions, too weak to engage in little more than futile protests and sporadic armed struggles. In other instances, the breakup of the colonizing state and the loss of the territory left the settlers in a precarious situation—no matter whether a result of defeat by outside powers in the case of Japan, the disintegration of the state from within in the case of the Soviet Union, or a "liberation" struggle by the occupied peoples in the case of Algeria. Japan removed its settlers from Manchuria following its defeat; the *pieds noirs* fled Algeria to resettle in France; however, the bulk of the Russian-speakers (an estimated 25 million) remained in the "near abroad," those states previously part of the Soviet empire. The primary political and social effects of many of these colonization policies were upon the countries of origin, or in the case of the Russians, upon the settlers themselves and their relationship with the host governments.

In other instances the native populations of the settled areas fled, particularly when the settlement process generated armed conflict with the local population. Again, examples abound: conflicts and refugee flights among the Bengali-speaking Muslims in Burma, the Buddhists in Bangladesh's Chittagong Hill Tracts, and Tibetans in southwest China. The imposition of settlers upon a native population often resulted in conflicts with neighboring countries as refugees fled across international borders.[3]

There are also numerous cases of conflicts between settlers and the native population, or between a native population and a government perceived as an occupier, when both natives and settlers choose to remain *in situ*. Contemporary cases include the Palestinians in relation to the government of Israel and the Jewish settlers; Uighurs in relation to the government of China and to the Han settlers; Moros in relation to the government of Philippines and the Christian settlers; various ethnic groups in Sumatra, East Timor, and Irian Jaya in relation to the settlers and to the government of Indonesia; Albanians of Kosovo in relation to the Serbs and to the Serb government; Kurds in Western Anatolia in relation to Turk settlers and to the government of Turkey. One should also include Russians living in Estonia, Kazakhstan, and several other former republics, where the government of Russia has been pressing for dual citizenship for the Russian-speaking population living in the "near abroad." In none of these cases has there been a mass exodus, although one should quickly add "thus far" to remind us of how politically and demographically fragile is each of these regions.

Settlement policies thus affect two communities—settlers and natives—and two governments: the host government, and the government and country to which either the settlers or the natives are forced or choose to move. Settlement policies enable a government to establish control over a territory, but the costs can be high: hostile relations between the settlers and the natives, and strained relations with one's neighbors if there are forced deportations. To maintain settler control over an area with a large indigenous population, a high element of coercion is required. Secessionist and irredentist movements must be crushed, protest movements put down. There is little space available for political democratization that would enable the natives to take matters into their own hands and impose restrictions upon the settlers. If and when democratization does take place, then settlers are at risk—as they are in Baltic states, as they would be if China democratized Tibet and Xinjiang, and when a democratic Indonesian government gives free choice to East Timor and some of the other outer islands with large settler populations.

The movement of one people to the space occupied by another does not in itself necessarily provoke an antagonistic reaction. The central question is whether the local population feels that another population has been imposed upon it, that is, that the settler population represents a conquering power. Under these circumstances the settler population, while a demographic minority, is likely to refuse to be incorporated into the native culture and social order. In turn, the native population—even when the settler population is large—is likely to resist the "tipping" phenomenon, the point at which individuals in a community change their behavior by moving or by assimilating—because they believe that other members of their own community will change their behavior. Tipping is not likely to take place when one community looks upon another as its nemesis—a long-standing rival or enemy whose presence in the territory constitutes a threat to one's culture, social structure, and perhaps even to one's safety.

Under these circumstances the "will to difference," to use Charles Taylor's appropriate phrase (Taylor et al. 1994), is likely to be intense. The native population becomes bound together by its vision of the settlers as a people imposed upon them and of themselves as the victims of oppression, tied together by shared suffering, shared humiliation, and a shared "private" history that must now be hidden from the occupiers. The native population does not regard the settler population merely as migrants, but as occupiers, whose presence is made possible by the political power of a center—Paris, Beijing, Manila, Rangoon, Moscow, Jakarta, Jerusalem—and so their wrath, private or public, is directed not only at the settlers but at the political center. Under these circumstances natives demand autonomy, independence, self-determination, and other measures aimed at restoring their dignity, ending their humiliation, and "returning" to them, as it were, a sense of control over their land and over themselves.

The "will to difference," so characteristic of all nationalist sentiments, is particularly acute for those who regard themselves as a suffering, humiliated people by virtue of the presence of an imposed settler population. Under these circumstances many of the processes that often obtain between locals and migrants—integration, intermarriage, assimilation, the blurring of differences, the mutual sharing of culture, political accommodation—are resisted and the will to difference is accentuated. The natives may learn the language of the settlers—Uighurs learn Chinese, Estonians learn Russian, Kosovars learn Serbo-Croatian, Chakmas learn Bengali, Rohingyas learn Burmese—but the settlers resist learning the language of the natives. The acquisition by the natives of the settler language does not involve the replacement of the mother tongue but is adopted as a means of dealing with the enemy and with authority.

Settlers, whose migration is motivated by official encouragement, thus differ from migrants in several critical ways. One is that settlers regard themselves as superior to the natives and do not wish to be incorporated into the native culture or to acquire its language. Another is that the natives develop an acute "will to difference." They may learn the language of the settlers, but use their native tongue with one another and not with the settlers. Language and history become interiorized. The native population propagate their language, their culture, their history upon immigrants, but not upon settlers. Settlers are not initially threatened by the local culture; their principal fear is that they will be deserted by the ruling authority that has enabled or encouraged them to come.

The removal of the ruling authority—the departure, for example, of France from Algeria, the Soviet Union from the non-Russian states, the Japanese from Manchuria, the Portuguese from Angola and Mozambique—invariably creates a crisis in the relationship between the native population (now the ruling authority) and the settlers, who have now become politically subordinate. Should the settlers exit? If they choose to stay, do they remain an enclave emphasizing their own "will to difference"? Should they learn the local language and attempt to accommodate themselves to a politically subordinate role? Should they adopt measures to encourage higher birth rates, thereby exercising a kind of "strategic demography"? How the settlers and the native population cope with the new political situation depends upon their numbers, their concentration and location, and their respective places in the occupational structure and in the economy.

Demographic Engineering and Security

To engineer, as a transitive verb, is to lay out, to construct, to manage: One engineers a bill through Congress; the state can also engineer the movement of people. The implication of the notion of demographic engineering, therefore, is that the movement of peoples is not the consequence of social and economic trends— such as differentials in wages or employment opportunities across regions. Nor does demographic engineering refer to all actions by the state that result in the large-scale movement of populations—for example, the failure of government to deal with a famine, or the neglect of the environment, or the construction of a large dam which will displace a segment of society. Demographic engineering implies that the movement itself is deliberately induced by the state; it is not the consequence of another policy or program. The political reasons for inducing movement and what policy instruments are utilized vary. The instruments are on a continuum, ranging from the use of military force to deport a population—round them up, terrorize and/or humiliate them, put them on trains or trucks—to the opening of agricultural lands, the provision of loans and subsidies to encourage outsiders to settle.

Why is demographic engineering of interest from a security perspective? Demographic engineering policies often generate hostility not only among peoples but toward the state itself. Deported populations are invariably resentful at having been uprooted from their territorial homeland and for generations may seek to be reunited with their native land. In this sense, of course, land is not simply property with market value, but a place to which one is emotionally attached. It is not simply land, but a *home*land.

Colonizers, in contrast, are not necessarily hostile to the state— indeed, they may be pleased that new opportunities for land or employment at high wages have been provided. It is the host population, the natives, who turn against the state for having brought in outsiders. The very presence of settlers is a constant reminder that the policies once adopted by the state were illegitimate and that perhaps the state itself remains illegitimate. The natives may thus turn against both the settlers and the state. Just as deported people may for generations long to return to their native land, so too a native population may for generations resent the presence of a people whom they regard as colonizers. At some point in time, of course, a deported people may, as it were, give up, or a native population may either absorb or be absorbed by the colonizers, but the process is likely to be long and contentious.

Once again it is necessary to remind ourselves that these processes have significant international consequences. The native population may launch a secessionist movement, a civil war that invites international attention and external intervention. Settlers and natives may engage in a political struggle that leads to armed conflict. Natives or settlers may flee across international borders to seek asylum, thereby generating conflicts with a neighboring country and engaging the attention of international human rights and refugee organizations. Minorities, whether deported populations or native populations, invariably seek support from their co-ethnics elsewhere. The Great Game, the most effective weapon of the weak (Rubinstein 1983), is to internationalize domestic conflicts.

Notes

1. The particular use of the word "settlers" here should be distinguished from another usage in discussions of migration, which refers to that fraction of temporary international migrants who "settle out" and become permanent residents.
2. For a more detailed study, see Banister (2001: 287).
3. For a study of this area, see Tirtosudarmo (2001).

— *Six* —

POPULATION UNMIXING

———⟨⟨∅∅∅⟩⟩———

The unmixing of peoples, or what is now pejoratively described as "ethnic cleansing," can be the result of a government policy, the outcome of an extended historical process, or a combination of the two. Cities, regions, entire countries have been demographically transformed as much by the exodus of populations as by in-migration. Places that were once demographically predominantly of one "people"—it is easy to slip into an essentialist language—can be transformed as their populations move elsewhere. This chapter describes some of the major instances of population unmixing, why they occurred, the circumstances under which the process is seen as threatening, and to whom.

The origins of the "ethnic cleansing" terminology, so closely associated with the 1990s wars in the former Yugoslavia, is itself clouded in ambiguity. Some attribute its first use to the contested region of Nogorno-Karabakh in Azerbaijan. Others point to Croatia: William Safire (1993) quotes a Serbian building supervisor living in Croatia in July 1991: "Many of us have been sacked because they want an ethnically clean Croatia." In the same month, Croatia's Supreme Council alleged that Serbian expulsions of Croats was aimed at "the ethnic cleansing of the critical areas ... to be annexed to Serbia." A *New York Times* correspondent in the former Yugoslavia observed in July 1992 that the "precondition" for the creation of a "Greater Serbia" "lies in the purging—ethnic cleansing, in the perpetrators' lexicon—of wide areas of Bosnia" (Wohlstetter 1994).

The Yugoslavian disasters have made the term "ethnic cleansing" part of the vernacular: An ethnically mixed population can be "purified" by changing the demographics through expulsion of the "undesirable" population from a given territory. The strategy is a politics of terror sufficiently powerful to convince people to abandon their homes and land to others; the tools of choice are shelling of civilians, murder, rape, intimidation, humiliation, and torture, justified by "religious or ethnic discrimination, political, strategic or ideological conditions or a combination of these" (Bell-Fialkoff 1993).

Yet whatever the origins of the terminology, the contemporary humanitarian disasters of the former Yugoslavia are hardly unique. The Nazis' original efforts to make Germany *Judenrein* (free of Jews) was a policy of "ethnic cleansing." Others include the forced relocation of Native Americans in the nineteenth century, and of Armenians from the Ottoman Empire in 1915. In both cases, thousands of men, women, and children were forcibly expelled from their homelands under conditions of appalling brutality (Winter 1994).

After World War II, the forced relocation of ethnic Germans living in Russia, Poland, and Czechoslovakia was driven by revenge and fear on the part of both the victorious Allies and the newly formed governments in some of these countries (see the discussion later in this chapter). The huge migrations in both directions which accompanied the partition of British India in 1947, initially a planned effort to protect both Hindus and Muslims from religious/ethnic extremists, were ultimately overwhelmed by mass terror. The flight of Palestinians from what is now Israel during the 1947–48 Middle East War resulted from mass fear, some of it cultivated by Israelis, some by Arabs, some resulting simply from the fog of war (Morris 1987). What made the "ethnic cleansings" in the Yugoslavian civil wars distinctive was their deliberate calculation as a political strategy based upon the maximization of fear.

Consider also the exodus of Christians from the Middle East, the historic homeland of Christianity. Conflicts between Christian communities, the movement of Ottoman Turks into Asia Minor, the growth of Islamic militancy, as well as Israeli policies toward Palestinians, have all had the effect of reducing the presence of Christians throughout the region. Alexandria, once a thriving center for Greek culture and a major Jewish and Armenian settlement so memorably captured in Lawrence Durrell's *Alexandria Quartet*, is no longer a great multi-cultural center, a focal point for the cosmopolitanism of the Mediterranean, but a provincial Egyptian city.

A similar demographic de-cosmopolitanization has taken place in Beirut. The Lebanese civil war, in which Christians fought Christians,[1] led an estimated quarter of the Maronite community in Lebanon to flee the Middle East—to Israel, the United States, Canada, and Australia. A similar exodus of Christians, notably the Armenians and Greek Pontic communities, has been going on for centuries throughout the Black Sea region, but it accelerated with the breakup of the Ottoman Empire and the emergence of the modern Turkish state and its Armenian genocide. The exodus of Palestinian Christians from Israel, which began in 1948, accelerated after 1967, so that now a majority of Palestinian Christians live outside of Israel. The historic Armenian quarter of Jerusalem is losing population as its younger residents emigrate to the West and to Australia: Boston, New York, and Sydney have become favorite destinations. The Jewish quarter of Jerusalem, once a "mixed neighborhood," is becoming exclusively Jewish as settlers buy land and homes formerly owned by Christians and Muslims. In Egypt the growth of militant Islamic movements has put the Coptic Christians at risk, and there has been a movement of Coptic farmers from Upper Egypt into the cities, while large numbers of Coptic professionals have left for Australia, Canada, and the United States.

As Christians have emigrated from the Middle East, so have the Jews: Historic demographic and cultural centers in North Africa, Iraq, Iran, and Syria have become devoid of Jews. There has been a reconfiguration of Jews in Israel; it is a very different Jewish population from the one that resided in Palestine in the nineteenth century and earlier. In the Middle East today, it is principally Syria that retains a significant Jewish-Muslim-Christian mix, but given the precarious character of its political leadership, it seems unlikely that the mix will be sustained for long.

The unmixing of peoples or "ethnic cleansing" also entails the destruction of archeological remains, places of worship, cemeteries, and other physical and cultural sites that enable people to recall the presence of a people who have since been removed. One scholar provides a vivid account of the destruction of Armenian sites in the Middle East:

As my friend George Hintlian, curator of the Armenian Museum in Jerusalem put it: "You can attribute disappearing churches to earthquakes, robbers, Kurds, Islamic fundamentalists, men from outer space or anything else you care to blame. The end result is exactly the same. Every passing year another Armenian church disappears and for this the Turkish authorities can only be pleased. They have already changed all the Armenian village names in eastern Anatolia; the churches are all we have left. Soon there will be virtually no evidence that the Armenians were ever in Turkey. We will have become a historical myth." (Dalrymple 1988: 88)

Such efforts to erase visible elements of unwanted cultures have been particularly evident in the ethnic cleansing that has occurred in the former Yugoslavia—in Bosnia, in Croatia, in Kosovo alike. Targets of such destruction have included the famous museum in Sarajevo, not to mention numerous mosques and churches.

The unmixing of populations, as Rogers Brubaker argues in his excellent study (Brubaker 1996: 148–178), is one of the major demographic consequences of the breakup of empires. In large part this is because state-sponsored migrations are frequently key instruments in the making of empires. Brubaker reminds us of the steps taken by the pre-Soviet Russian regime and then by the Soviet government to extend their control through settlement policies to promote the movement of non-Russians: the settlement of German colonists in the lower Volga, the emigration of Circassians, the deportation of Karachai, Kalmyks, Chechen, Ingush, Balkars, and Crimean Tatars for their alleged collaboration during World War II. Although much of the concern over the unmixing of populations in the post-Soviet state has focused on the 25 million Russians living outside of Russia, Brubaker points to other post-imperial migrations: Muslim/Turkish migration along ethnoreligious rather than ethnolinguistic lines from the Balkans following the disintegration of the Ottoman Empire; the Magyar migration from the Hungarian successor states after the collapse of the Habsburg Empire in World War I; and an influx of Germans into Germany from territories ceded to Poland.

The unmixing of populations in Central and Eastern Europe which accelerated after World War II continues to the present. There was large-scale consolidation of the German-speaking population in Europe after 1945, in part the result of the redrawn borders of Central and Eastern Europe, and in part the consequence of the forced movement of German-speaking minorities into Germany. Millions of people of German descent in Central and Eastern Europe were expelled from their homes, lost their property, and fled west. There are conflicting estimates as to the numbers involved. The first group—the *Reichsdeutsche*, or Germans in the eastern provinces of East Prussia, Eastern Pomerania, Eastern Brandenburg, and Silesia—had numbered over nine million in 1939; following the postwar redrawing of the borders of Poland, Russia, and Hungary, most were forced to move westward into occupied Germany proper. The second group—the *Volksdeutsche*, or Germans living as minorities in Czechoslovakia, Poland, Hungary, Yugoslavia, and Romania—numbered another seven million. These were the so-called "fifth column" of ethnic minority Germans, who after the depredations of the war were no longer welcome in the successor states of 1945. Between 1945 and 1950 about three million were expelled from Czechoslovakia and nearly two million from other countries. A third group was the *lebensraum* colonizers—some one million *Volksdeutsche* and *Reichsdeutsche* the Nazis had sent to settle parts of Poland, Yugoslavia, and Russia, and who were evacuated by the German army during their retreat from the east in 1944–45.

In all, perhaps 12 million Germans were forced out of their homes. The victorious Allies agreed to the principle of mass population transfers in 1944, and during the five years after the end of the war they implemented this policy. The result was a dramatically new ethnic map of Europe—substantially but hardly entirely unmixed. In particular, large regions of eastern Europe, sites of centuries-old German civilization, were transformed root and branch by mass expropriations of German property and land. Perhaps two million people of German descent died in the flight and expulsion, and the survivors have never forgotten the trauma. About one-quarter of the population of the two Germanys in the 1960s had been forced to move west to the borders of the new German states: over 11 million residents of West Germany and 3.5 million residents of East Germany in 1966 (Teitelbaum and Winter 1998: 18–19). Later, beginning in the 1960s and continuing to the present, the remaining ethnic German populations in countries such as Romania, and in the Soviet Union and its successor states, were also encouraged to move to Germany, with Romania successfully demanding a hard-currency fee for each ethnic German allowed to leave. Brubaker (1996: 166) concludes: "As a result, the once-vast German diaspora of Eastern

Europe and Russia is today undergoing a rapid, and probably final dissolution."

Most scholars of the post-Soviet state do not anticipate any further large-scale emigration to Russia of Russian-speakers from the successor states. In the main, economic opportunities for Russian-speakers remain greater outside of than within Russia. Moreover, the successor non-Russian states with large Russian-speaking populations—the Baltic Republics, Kazakhstan, and the Ukraine—have largely been solicitous of the concerns of their Russian minorities on migration, citizenship, and language policies, although at times the relationships have been problematic. But one could readily imagine circumstances that would lead to a significant exodus—clashes between the Russian settler population and Kazakhs in Kazakhstan, a political (and violent) breakdown in Ukraine, or the growth of anti-Russian sentiment in any of the successor states that would affect everyday life of Russians and instill a fear of violence or diminished opportunities.[2]

Migration from the former Soviet republics to Russia is by no means confined to the Russian-speaking population. There have been significant flows of non-Russian nationalities (Armenians, Meshkhetian Turks, Azerbaijani refugees from Armenia and Nagorno-Karabakh) to the Russian Federation. Civil conflicts in Abhkhazia, Chechnya, and Tadzhikistan have resulted in refugee flows to Ukraine, Kazakstan, Belarus, the Russian Federation, and to other former Soviet republics. In the 1980s, some the peoples deported by Stalin's regime—Crimean Tatars, Meshkhetians, and Volga Germans—started to return to their historic homelands, and this migratory flow continues. The present trend is one of greater Russification of the European republics and a greater indigenization of the non-European republics, but given the political and economic upheavals underway it would be premature to predict what the ethnic configurations of the successor states will be in a generation.

What is clear, however, is that the Russian Federation may be in the midst of a historic demographic decline, unless current low fertility rates rebound dramatically from levels that have been depressed by economic and political turmoil. The latest UN demographic projections show the Russian population declining from 148 million in 1995 to 138 million in 2025 (medium-variant) with a low-to-high-variant range from 131 to 150 million for the same year (United Nations 1999: 352–353). Russia is now smaller than Indonesia, Brazil, or Pakistan (United Nations 1998: 3); the

Russian GNP per capita is below that of Brazil, Mexico, South Africa, Malaysia, South Korea, and other upper middle-income developing countries, with a declining role in the global economy. The process of unmixing peoples through emigration so characteristic of post-colonial regimes, combined with low and declining population growth and an imploding economy, would relegate Russia to Third-World status were it not for its weapons of mass destruction, its geopolitical position in the Eurasian heartland, and a history that bespeaks a powerful capacity for regeneration.

Our last example of population unmixing within Europe is in the Balkans, where the breakup of Yugoslavia resulted in the reconfiguration of populations in the five successor states of Bosnia, Slovenia, Croatia, Macedonia, and the rump Federal Republic of Yugoslavia (Serbia and Montenegro). Most of the successor states and the European powers have verbally stood fast against the notion of ethnic cleansing, and the Dayton Accord rejected both ethnic cleansing and proposals to redraw international borders to create greater homogeneity among the successor states, yet in reality an unmixing of religious and linguistic groups has occurred such that each of the successor units is more homogeneous than it had been prior to the breakup. Indeed, while there are five successor states, on the ground there are, in effect, nine ethnically defined regions.[3] While the Bosnian Muslims want a multi-ethnic state, other ethnic and religious communities have sought ethnic separation.

Principal (and principled) opposition to partition and separation for Bosnia has come from the United States, where a deep liberal commitment to ethnic mixing prevails. The Dayton Accord demographically partitioned Bosnia into areas of ethnic homogeneity by the way in which the de facto borders were drawn, but resisted the notion that Bosnia should be broken into separate sovereign states, with its territory and population doled out, as it were, to its various ethnic neighbors. The United States and its allies, concerned over still further disintegration (as with the possible withdrawal of Montenegro) and additional ethnic cleansing, have long opposed independence for Kosovo from Serbia. In 1999, these matters came to a violent head, with Serbian forces brutally attempting to "cleanse" Kosovo of the estimated 90 percent of its population who were ethnically Albanian. This led to a concerted military intervention by NATO, which was ended by a Serbian agreement to withdraw its forces and allow what amounted to a military takeover of the province by

NATO forces. The future status of Kosovo, whether as an independent state or a self-governing region nominally still part of Serbia, remains in doubt as of this writing, although it seems almost certain to be under international trusteeship for a substantial period into the future.

This brief overview of the process of ethnic unmixing in postcolonial and post-ethnic-conflict societies suggests a demographic reality that is at variance with normative preferences. While neither the breakup of multi-cultural empires nor violent conflict in multi-ethnic states is inevitable, once conflict or disintegration does take place there is a very high probability that ethnic/religious minority communities will emigrate. There may be several options on the ground: migration across national borders to another country where there is a dense concentration of one's ethnic group; flight to any country that can provide sanctuary; or demographic (but not necessarily political) partition within the country. The demographic outcomes are often similar: the unmixing of people in what were once diverse religious or linguistic communities where they lived, if not in harmony, at least side by side, intermingling in their daily lives.

This question of whether it is desirable to separate people engaged in violent conflict or to attempt to facilitate their (re)integration is one of the most contentious of many of the still-unresolved policy debates in this domain. It arises with greatest force in states or regions characterized by ethnically intermixed patterns of residence, coupled with a history of enmity or nationalism among two or more of the ethnic groups involved such that more than one lays claim to a homeland or territory (Nichiporuk 2000). If in such a setting an ethnic conflict emerges and escalates into serious violence involving ethnic cleansing or genocide, the question arises as to whether the groups should be separated through some form of political autonomy, partition, or transfer of territory from one sovereign to another.

The issue is invariably shrouded in moral preferences: To accede to partition after acts of genocide, pogroms, and forced population movements, it is often argued, is to legitimize ethnic cleansing. Critics, on the other hand, point to the risks of sending refugee minorities back home to communities where the level of violence has been high and when they continue to be at risk. Should governments and international organizations (including the UNHCR) for example promote the repatriation of Serbs to Muslim or Croat-controlled areas of Bosnia, Bosnian Muslims to

Serb-controlled areas of Bosnia, or Tutsi to Rwanda, and set out to create institutions (a reformed police system, tribunals for dealing with violations of human rights, a restructured electoral system, and so on) that would bring divided communities together? Alternatively, should outsiders attempt to negotiate some form of separation through autonomy or partition? With the exception of a handful of empirical studies of the consequences of these alternatives (for example, Kaufmann 1996a, 1996b; 1998), the debate largely lies in the realm of normative preferences.

The current worldwide trend toward demographic unmixing runs counter to a prevailing view that the globalization process and global migration *reduces* the importance of borders and enables people to migrate more freely to areas of economic opportunity with little regard for differences in language, culture, or indeed citizenship. From this latter perspective the model is, or should be, traditional migration countries—the United States, Canada, Australia, and now the new centers of migration in Western Europe. In the old and "new" immigration countries the issues are citizenship, language, education, employment policies, and neighborhood integration—all amid a debate over cultural pluralism.

It has been the thesis of this chapter, however, that for much of the world the demographic tendencies have been toward ethnic consolidation rather than diversification, and that the demographic processes of exodus and return have resulted in increasing homogeneity along religious, linguistic, and other ethnic lines. It is premature to say that there is a global trend in one direction or another—indeed, one should assume great regional and national variability—but it is striking how powerful are the forces that push countries toward some form of ethnic consolidation.

One critical factor is that governments and ethnic majority leaders often regard earlier migrations as having been illegitimate. When imperial regimes engage in demographic engineering by permitting or inducing settlers to enter, the indigenous population, faced with an immigrant population that speaks another language, worships other gods, and competes for land and jobs, is likely to hold the view that this imported population does not fully belong there. Under these circumstances it is likely that the local population will develop an ideology, as it were, of "indigenousness," the notion that there is a special tie between the indigenes and the land. Governments of multi-ethnic societies resist this claim by putting forth a counterposition: that in a multi-ethnic society people should be free to move to where economic opportunities are present and should even be induced to move in order to promote national integration. Thus, the government of Indonesia promotes the movement of people from densely populated Java to the outer islands, China promotes the migration of Han peoples to Tibet and Xinjiang provinces, the government of Brazil encourages migration to its forest-rich western territories, and throughout the nineteenth century the United States promoted migration into territories occupied by Native Americans and by Mexicans.

As we have noted earlier, both these two claimants—settlers and indigenous peoples—have developed their own ideological positions, reached out to international civil society for support, nurtured ties to the global media, and created alliances with co-ethnics that offer the prospect for financial as well as political support. In these circumstances there is a high potential for violent conflict.

Notes

1. While the popular percepton of the Lebanese civil war was one of Christian against Muslim, in fact Christians also fought other Christians, and Muslims fought other Muslims.
2. As John Harris of Boston University has noted, if countries treat their minorities badly enough, the international community may be willing to do the engineering for them via the refugee system.
3. For a particularly fine analysis of the breakup of Yugoslavia and its consequences, see Ash (1999).

— *Seven* —

DIASPORAS
Whom Do They Threaten?

In many, perhaps most, of the world's countries, there are significant resident ethnic communities produced by historical and contemporary migrations. Some of these populations may appropriately be characterized as "diasporas"[1]—peoples who are settled far from their ancestral homelands. Examples abound in the modern world: Armenian, Irish, Russian, Albanian, African (from a variety of modern countries), Lebanese, Kurdish, Jewish, Arab, Tamil, Sikh, Vietnamese, Cambodian, Cuban, Haitian, and many others.

Many members of these diasporic groups feel understandable links of kinship, or at least of symbolic affinity, to the regions and countries from which they or their ancestors came. These connections are normally benign—interest in the affairs of the "homeland," affiliation into ethnic organizations such as churches and schools; financial remittances sent in support of kinsman still in the homeland; even investment there in businesses and land.

Yet in addition to these there can be connections tied to violence: Some members of these communities, out of sympathy for the cause of their brethren in their "home" country, can be mobilized to provide financial help to groups associated with "freedom fighters" or "terrorists" (depending upon one's orientation to a particular situation). Remittances flow from overseas diasporas to the Tamil Tigers (LTTE) in Sri Lanka, the IRA in northern Ireland, the Albanian Liberation Front (ALF) in Kosovo, Hamas in Gaza and the West Bank, making it possible for combatants to buy sophisticated arms such as shoulder-firing, heat-seeking surface-to-air missiles, Kalashnikoff assault rifles, walkie-talkies, grenades, and materials for the construction of explosive devices, all of which are available through the world's small-weapons market. In some cases, financial support from overseas diasporas is only a small financial source for these movements; often, few of the contributors are aware of the ultimate use of their contributions, since the checks they write are to *bona fide* tax-exempt charitable organizations purportedly providing support for health and educational services abroad.

We do not know, nor can we ever know, how much money goes from the diasporas to religious fundamentalist, secessionist, irredentist, radical, liberationist, and other causes. What we do know is that the scale of these movements and their capacity to buy weapons depends upon their finances, and while they can sustain themselves through the sale of drugs, tithing their supporters, and from contributions from friendly governments, many depend heavily upon contributions from their overseas supporters. Among the armed groups that depend upon external support, some from governments and some more than others from migrant communities abroad, are: the Motherland Party and other Islamic groups in Turkey; the Kurdistan Worker's Party (PKK) operating in Turkey, Iraq, and Syria; the Sikh Khalistan movement in India's Punjab; the Popular Front for the Liberation of Palestine (PFLP) in Syria; the Moro National Liberation Front (MNLF) in the Philippines; the East Timor Liberation movement in Indonesia; the National Liberation Front (FMLN) in El Salvador; the Muhajir Quami Mahaz (MQM) party in Karachi.

The anti-regime activities of the migrants can threaten the homeland not only because of the money they provide for the purchase of weapons, but also through their access to the global media and their capacity to bring the cause of a minority community to the attention of governments and international non-governmental organizations. Politically weak anti-regime movements need international support for their cause; it is therefore in their interest to internationalize their demands.

The governments and especially the security agencies of the United States, Canada, Germany, France, the Netherlands, Great

Britain, and other Western countries are concerned that their migrant communities may constitute a security threat by virtue of their transnational identities. The reality, however, is that migrant communities—to the extent that they constitute a threat—have more often been a threat to the governments of their country of origin than to their country of residence. To be sure, there have been spillovers from the politics of the homeland— conflicts between Turks and Kurds in Germany, Hindus and Muslims in the UK, bombing of synagogues in Buenos Aires and Istanbul, and terrorist attacks in France, the Netherlands, Canada, and on New York's World Trade Center. Threatening as these actions have been, the number of people engaged in them is small, and there is no evidence that they have popular support. Some members of the diaspora may engaged in violent acts against a host government whose policies toward their country of origin they oppose, but these have never become and are unlikely to become mass movements. The risk, rather, is a back-lash against migrants and refugees, the growth of anti-migrant, anti-foreign sentiment that under some conditions may take a repressive, anti-democratic form.

All things considered, modern democratic states are likely to find that their immigrant/refugee populations do not constitute a significant threat to their domestic security. To the extent that diaspora communities are engaged in actions that constitute a security threat, it is largely to provide support for violent and radical movements in their country of origin rather than in their host society: Germany is a financial center for Islamic funda-mentalists in Turkey and France for Islamic fundamentalists in Algeria; Sinhalese Tamils work out of several European coun-tries as well as from the United States; Sikh activists are head-quartered in Canada. Supporters of radical Irish groups have been based in the United States; Albanian supporters of the Kosovo Liberation Front worked out of Switzerland and Italy as well as the United States.

There are two circumstances under which a diaspora commu-nity is likely to take up anti-regime activities toward its country of origin. The first is when a section of the diaspora shares an identity with a secessionist ethnic minority in the country of ori-gin, for example Tamils in Sri Lanka, Kosovars in Yugoslavia, Sikhs and Kashmiris in India, Biafrans in Nigeria, Eritreans in Ethiopia, Kurds in Iraq. Although some governments may be sympathetic to secessionist movements, few governments are willing actively to take up the cause of a secessionist diaspora: It does, after all, constitute a form of intervention in the affairs of another state. But there is often popular sympathy in the host society for "self-determination," especially for a repressed people who appear to be victims of an aggressive nationalist movement.

The second is when the diaspora, confident of the support or at least non-interference of the host country, supports political movements at home that seek to overthrow an existing regime. Diaspora communities based in the United States have been particularly active in support of movements to overthrow dictatorships in the home country: the Marcos regimes in the Philippines, the military government in Nigeria, the apartheid government in South Africa, the Indira Gandhi government during the Emergency, the authoritarian government in South Korea. Many of these political movements received political support from their host government and the media. Diaspora support for these movements, therefore, has not been regarded as threatening to the host society.

Why diaspora communities often support militant movements in their homeland when they have settled in and even acquired citizenship elsewhere is an interesting psychological phenomenon. For some the motivation is guilt, for others it is a way of assuaging the pain of departure from one's country and people by providing support for those who embody the most intense form of ethnic identity. Support for ethnic militants is a way of holding on to an identity even as one assimilates to a new culture and new language. Members of the diaspora may be angry at regimes that are oppressing their people and from which many of the immigrants fled as refugees. What this anger rarely represents, however, is hostility or disloyalty to the country of immigration.

It is noteworthy that no immigrant community in the United States or Europe has formed a political party directed against its host society, notwithstanding substantial pockets of alienation among many North Africans in France and Turks in Germany. In the United States diaspora communities take up causes related to the government of the country from which they come— Greek-Americans oppose aid to Turkey, Asian Indians take up issues involving Pakistan, Cuban-Americans oppose Castro— but these claims are part of American interest-group politics, and have not been regarded as a threat to U.S. security. The new question is whether dual nationality or dual citizenship changes the dynamics in the relationship between diaspora communities and governments by posing issues of loyalty. It is to these issues that we now turn.

The Looming National Debates over Dual Citizenship

In a ceremony at the National Palace in Mexico in June 1998, President Ernesto Zedillo presented the first of twelve certificates of nationality under a newly approved law that allows people to hold citizenship abroad without losing Mexican nationality. Under the new legislation Mexicans who had given up their citizenship, including millions who have become American citizens, became eligible to regain their Mexican nationality. The first in line, according to the Associated Press (4 June 1998), was Professor Mario Molina of the Massachusetts Institute of Technology, winner of the 1995 Nobel Prize for Chemistry.

The new law eliminated the loss of Mexican inheritance and property rights that previously faced those taking foreign citizenship. It did not, however, grant voting rights to nationals abroad, or permit nationals abroad to hold most public offices in Mexico. The law allows émigrés and their foreign-born children to "recover" Mexican nationality by producing a birth certificate or other related documents and paying a small fee. Among the benefits of this form of dual citizenship is that the children of immigrants will be able to attend state-funded universities in Mexico, which charge nominal tuition. The legislation also provided that Mexicans who become naturalized citizens of another country will no longer automatically lose their Mexican nationality. Supporters of the legislation argued that the major practical effect would be to boost applications for U.S. citizenship by Mexicans, thereby both enhancing their political rights and increasing the political power of Mexican-Americans in U.S. domestic and foreign policies.

Other countries have also passed legislation permitting some form of dual citizenship or dual nationality. Colombia, the Dominican Republic, Israel, and Ireland preceded Mexico in extending nationality to émigrés, though the presence of an estimated seven million Mexican-born immigrants in the United States makes this the most consequential case of dual citizenship or dual nationality. The Mexican law distinguishes between "nationality" and "citizenship" by granting émigrés economic and social rights as Mexican nationals but not granting them the right to vote or to hold political office. In practice, however, dual nationals could vote in Mexican federal elections as long as they registered and cast their ballots in Mexico.

The concept and practice of dual citizenship is by no means new. Ascherson (1995) argues that "the notion that nation-states had a right and even a duty to extend some degree of member-ship to their own ethnic compatriots abroad" was an expression of post-1918 nationalism.

> Cultural affinity was to be developed into political affiliation. This idea was taken up principally by nations with a tradition of emigra-tion and a recognizable Diaspora. Germany, Ireland and finally Israel [and, one might now add, Italy and Japan] were among the nation-states which constructed versions of a "right to return," the right to citizenship based on ethnic criteria which could be biological, reli-gious, cultural or a mixture of all of them. (Ascherson 1995: 190–192)

Ascherson insightfully notes that as the cultural gap between the diaspora and the homeland widens, the subjective impor-tance of national identity may in some circumstances intensify: "This new diaspora patriotism may remain little more than a lux-ury of the imagination, but there are times when, suddenly and desperately, these cheques on the Bank of Symbolism are pre-sented for payment" (Asherson 1995).

Dual citizenship can be acquired by descent from parents who are nationals (*jus sanguinis*), by birth (*jus soli*) in a sovereign's ter-ritory, by marriage, by naturalization, or as a result of territorial transfers. The most common way in which dual citizenship is acquired is when individuals born in one country have parents who are citizens of another. What is new is that many govern-ments are now, as a matter of public policy, granting nationality or citizenship rights to their migrants abroad who have become citizens of another country. Their aim is to retain ties of affection between the migrants and their country of origin, typically so as to build or sustain an economic relationship—to encourage remittances (such as overseas workers' transfers of hard-cur-rency payments to family still in the home country), to generate investment by migrants in their country of origin, and to facili-tate the flow of technology. In some cases the goals also have a political complexion: to facilitate the growth of a voting bloc in the host country with interests and sympathies directed toward the country of origin, and to strengthen the civil and social rights of co-ethnics living in the country of immigration.

Citizenship implies obligations and allegiances. The "classic" view is that individuals swear allegiance to a sovereign and in return the sovereign provides protection to its citizens and subjects, including those who live abroad. According to this view individuals swear allegiance to only one sovereign; indeed, some countries require that individuals renounce prior allegiances as a condition for acquiring a new nationality. Naturalizing Americans are required to "abjure all allegiance and fidelity to any foreign prince, potentate, state or sovereignty, of whom or which I have heretofore been a subject or citizen."[2]

With a change in the circumstances under which individuals can now obtain dual citizenship, a variety of international conventions and treaties have been developed to address actual or potential conflicts. There are, for example, international agreements on military obligations of individuals who possess more than one nationality, conventions protecting the nationality of wives in the event of a dissolution of a marriage, and agreements for recognizing plural nationality. Although the United States formally insists upon exclusive allegiance, U.S. practices required by the Federal judiciary have in effect permitted dual citizenship. Similarly, the governments of other countries of immigration—Israel, Canada, Australia—have in practice permitted many of their citizens to retain their citizenship and passports of another country.

Are there circumstances under which dual nationality or dual citizenship constitutes a significant political or security problem for states? Most international lawyers say no. On the matter of voting by dual nationals, Aleinikoff and Klusmeyer (2001) conclude that "there is much less to these problems than meets the eye." However, critics of dual citizenship are concerned with the growing devaluation of citizenship in the United States and other democracies and its symbolic implications. For one thing, many immigrants now view citizenship less as a mark of allegiance than as a path to entitlements—to welfare, education, and other social benefits that states provide in larger measure to citizens than to non-citizens. In the U.S. case, such perceptions seem to have been enhanced by changes in eligibility for welfare benefits adopted under the welfare reform law of 1996. Citizenship also assures migrants that they have acquired the right to stay and to petition for the admission of others; indeed, for some, the acquisition of citizenship is motivated by the desire to bring other family members. For many businessmen of migrant origin, citizenship is also key to expanding opportunities for investment. The reverse is also true—investment has become a means of acquiring citizenship. Australia and Canada, among other countries, give "points" to investors, thereby offering them higher priority for immigrant admission and citizenship, and the United States allocates special visas for "investors" meeting certain criteria. From this perspective, the ultimate devaluation of citizenship is when it becomes a commodity, to be purchased by individuals for instrumental reasons.

Are there reasons to be alarmed by the growth of dual citizenship and by the devaluation of citizenship in many democratic states? First, it should be noted that for some countries citizenship is not being devalued, but rather becoming more intensely held, with rights and privileges tightly tied to citizenship. Concerned by the illegal movement of migrants across international borders, some states, including those in the Third World, are for the first time providing identity documents to their citizens and imposing tighter controls over borders. However, the growth in illegal migration and in the number of individuals who acquire dual citizenship can also be seen as still another demonstration that states are in fact losing control over their borders, of who enters, who acquires the right to remain, and who, as it were, "belongs" to the state.

One should not conclude, however, that states or borders are "withering away," for even as borders erode for some purposes—the flow of currencies, capital, and technology—they continue to be upheld for what most states regard as an essential core of their sovereignty, namely who is permitted entry, permanent residence, and citizenship. Still, the reality is that in North America and Europe older notions of citizenship and identity have eroded, and in their place some are promoting new notions of multi-culturalism, dual citizenship, dual nationality, and transnational identities.

In what sense, if at all, do these developments constitute a "threat" and, if so, to whom? Under what conditions, if any, might the native-born citizens of a country take objection to a growing number of dual citizens? Will there be a backlash from "native" Americans toward those who choose dual citizenship as somehow being less connected, less loyal (as some have alleged in the nuclear espionage scandal that engulfed the U.S. Department of

Energy in 1999)? Dual citizenship or dual nationality may not be regarded as threatening by American liberals committed to the idea of multi-culturalism, but that benign view may not be shared by all Americans.

Moreover, elsewhere in the world, dual citizenship may be regarded as particularly problematic in situations in which there are conflicts between migrant-receiving and migrant-sending countries, or between migrants and the citizens of their host country. Both in the past and in the present, such situations have sometimes been sources of conflict and violence. Consider, for example, the claims of Hungarian-speaking Transylvanians in Romania, Russian-speakers in eastern Estonia, ethnic Greeks in Albania, and scores of other peoples scattered throughout the successor states of the former Soviet Union. Then too there are the earlier claims of Sudetan Germans, French- and German-speaking populations in Alsace-Lorraine, Poles and Germans living throughout central and eastern Europe. Citizenship questions have been at issue in these conflicts, often part of larger questions of territorial boundaries, irredentist disputes, and demands for secession.

It is not difficult, however, to imagine conditions in which dual citizenship itself could become a matter of controversy. Were governments to permit dual citizenship of their own nationals to extend beyond the first generation of migrants and their children to successive generations, an enclave would be created that could be internally disruptive. Under such circumstances dual citizenship could slow the pace of immigrant integration and incorporation into American society of second and third generations of Mexican-Americans, or Russian-speakers in the case of the non-Russian successor states of the former Soviet Union, to give only two examples. Indeed, one can imagine a variety of dual nationality arrangements that are likely to pose issues between countries—Israeli-Arab citizens in a future Palestinian state; nationals of such a state who reside in Israel; Indonesia's Chinese as citizens of both countries; Nepali and Indian nationals who are citizens of both countries. Arrangements of this sort are increasingly likely, given the growth of national and international norms in support of minority rights and multiculturalism.

However, it is one thing for a population of migrant origin to feel a sense of cultural affinity to their country of origin, quite another to be citizens of that country and to be able to turn to another state to assert their cultural and political interests. Dual nationality gives individuals some claims upon their country of origin (such as the right to hold property, a second passport, free entry without visas, the right to invest on the same basis as other citizens in the country of origin, convertible bank accounts, and so on). The politically critical question is whether it also imposes some obligation on the government of the migrants' country of origin to protect their interests and security if they are threatened. Will the government of the country of origin make cultural claims on behalf of the migrants—for the right to maintain their own language, or for the right to separate schools, or for some form of affirmative action in admission to schools and colleges or in employment?

In the past the protection of one's citizens abroad has been regarded as an essential feature of national sovereignty. Looking to the future we can anticipate that an increasing number of minorities—both of indigenous and migrant origin—will make cultural claims upon their governments and will turn to any ethnic "home" government for support. Already, Mexican authorities have supported the claims of Mexican-Americans for social benefits; the Federal Republic of Germany has promoted the cultural interests of Germans in Kazakhstan and elsewhere in Eastern Europe; India is mindful of the interests of the Indian-origin and Tamil-speaking populations in Sri Lanka. In short, the "protection" of migrant and minority cultures by countries of origin is a likely new and expanding frontier for interventionist international politics.

Notes

1. Derived from the Greek *diaspeirein*, meaning dispersion. The word, when capitalized as in "the Diaspora," normally refers to the scattered colonies of Jews who settled around the world after their exile to Babylonia.
2. The entire U.S. Oath of Allegiance reads as follows: "I hereby declare, on oath, that I absolutely and entirely renounce and abjure all allegiance and fidelity to any foreign prince, potentate, state, or sovereignty of whom or which I have heretofore been a subject of citizen; that I will support and defend the Constitution and laws of the United States of America against all enemies, foreign and domestic; that I will bear true faith and allegiance to the same; that I will bear arms on behalf of the United States when required by the law; that I will perform noncombatant service in the Armed Forces of the United States when required by the law; that I will perform work of national importance under civilian direction when required by the law; and that I take this obligation freely without any mental reservation or purpose of evasion; so help me God."

— *Eight* —

THEORIES OF INTERNATIONAL MIGRATION AND THE ROLE OF THE STATE

Over the past decade, an extensive theoretical literature has been produced that seeks to explain the causes of observed patterns of international migration. Most has emerged from the disciplines of economics, demography, sociology, and geography. This chapter provides a very brief overview of current theoretical perspectives on international migration, and then addresses some of the main elements of actions taken by states insofar as they affect migration patterns. (For a discussion in greater depth, see Teitelbaum [2001].)

At the outset, it must be emphasized than none of these theoretical perspectives purports to explain or predict the movements of *bona fide* refugees. By definition, such persons are compelled to migrate across international boundaries due to persecution (on grounds specified in international agreements), and no existing social science model can adequately explain or predict such persecution. These theories do not address others who are not refugees but are forced to migrate to escape civil wars or natural catastrophes. There are other theoretical traditions, such as those in international relations that deal with causes of war, that are now in the early stages of considering the causes of such forced migrations, although it is only fair to acknowledge that most of these causes remain relatively opaque and unpredictable.

Economic Theories

One recent study of the economic literature on international migration[1] suggests that economic theories may usefully be grouped into five categories: neoclassical macroeconomic; neoclassical microeconomic; the "new economics of migration"; "dual labor market" theories; and "world systems" theories:

- The neoclassical macroeconomic perspective sees migration flows as driven by economic mechanisms that tend to equilibrate differentials between countries and regions that have substantial disparities in labor supply and demand.
- From the neoclassical microeconomic view, international migration is driven by decisions made by rational individuals who expect to gain positive net returns by moving to another country, taking into account both the benefits and costs involved; if the potential gains from migration increase while its costs are reduced by social, political, or technological developments, the volume of such migration will increase.
- The theories described by their authors as the "new economics of migration" focus on the social group or family unit rather than the individual. This group decides whether it is in the rational self-interest of the group for one of its members to migrate internationally. The goals may be not only to increase total group earnings, but also to diversify its earnings sources and thereby minimize its exposure to uncontrollable risks such as crop failure and local economic or political crises, and to gain access to capital and credit not locally available.
- In "dual labor market" theories, low-wage migrants are actively recruited by employers and governments in high-wage economies. The goals of such recruitment are to fill short-term "bottlenecks" in the labor market, to provide a contingent labor force that can be expanded or contracted in response to variation in demand, to "discipline" organized labor, and to restrain tendencies toward rising wages in tight labor markets.
- Finally, so-called "world systems" theories focus less on national economies and more on world markets, which produce international migration as capital and trade markets expand into "peripheral, noncapitalist societies." The

actors involved are less individuals and families, and more multinational firms, neocolonial governments, and national elites in peripheral societies.

Although some proponents put forward one or another of these economics-based approaches as sufficient explanations of migration behavior, none offers a convincing explanation on its own, although each provides useful insights.

Demographic Theories

Demographic interpretations also provide useful, if quite different, perspectives. Demographic forces described as important to the initiation of international movements include the following:

- high fertility and/or rapid population growth in source countries;
- low fertility and/or slow population growth in destination countries;
- the magnitudes of the differentials between two countries in such demographic rates;
- the indirect effects of demographic patterns on age composition, internal migration, urban unemployment, agrarian population densities, and environmental pressures.

Taken together, high fertility in some countries and low fertility in others produce what might be termed the *demographic differential hypothesis*, in which it is the magnitude and longevity of differential fertility rates between countries that substantially determine international population movements.

Proponents of this hypothesis[2] argue that if fertility rates below replacement level continue in many industrialized countries—mostly in Europe, but including Japan, Hong Kong, and Singapore—these countries will decline in demographic terms over the next quarter of a century, and will experience older populations and inflationary wage increases unless they admit large numbers of migrants from low-income, high-fertility areas. Low fertility rates also imply increases in the proportions beyond retirement age, imposing rising tax burdens on the working-age population if public pension systems are financed by pay-as-you-go taxation. In this analysis, then, imported workers serve the interests of employers (by holding down wage inflation) and of governments and older native populations (by slightly reducing the average population age and by increasing the number of workers contributing to financially insecure pay-as-you-go pension systems).

High-population-growth countries are, in contrast, likely to have an "excess" of young people in search of employment and therefore available for emigration. The high fertility and rapid population growth of much of the developing world leads to a kind of demographic "overspill," in which limits on available employment and resources impel some residents to seek better opportunities elsewhere. In addition, high fertility and population growth rates also produce, with roughly a two-decade lag, rapid growth in the numbers of young adults, a demographic category known to have the highest migration propensities.

This hypothesis thus postulates the existence of demographically "stagnant" and "dynamic" societies, which drives migration from the latter to the former. The demographic differential hypothesis thus challenges the most widely held migration theory, namely that international migration is principally driven by differential wages and employment opportunities.

A corollary of the differential fertility hypothesis is that in the absence of large-scale international migration, low-population-growth countries will experience a decline in their political power, since their diminished size will reduce their economic power, their share of world markets, and their capacity to wage war as a result of the declining number of young people and the reluctance of families to put their only sons in harm's way in combat. In contrast, demographically expanding countries, if their economies are also growing, will increase their global economic and political power. Demographically declining countries, from this perspective, must either import manpower or see their global economic and political power diminish (Wattenberg 1987).

There is, however, little or no evidence that differential fertility rates are currently driving international migration: Movement from one country to another does not appear to correlate with differential population growth rates. The major migration flows within Europe since the unification of Germany and the fall of the Soviet Union have been among countries with low fertility and low population growth rates, while in Africa and in much of the Third World the flows have been among countries with high fertility and population growth rates.

There are, to be sure, innumerable examples of migration flows from countries with high fertility to countries of low fertility: for example, from Central America and Mexico to the United States, from Tunisia and Morocco to Sicily, from North Africa to France, from Southeast Asia to Japan, and from Turkey and the successor states of Yugoslavia to Germany and Central Europe. But the flows among countries with high fertility rates continue unabated, as do the flows among countries with low fertility rates. The substantial migration flows within Southeast Asia, for example, or among the Central Asian republics of the former Soviet Union, or within Africa, are in the main among regions with similar (high or low) population growth rates.

Differential rates of fertility and population growth have not, as yet, been a major driving force in international migration. The flows continue to be shaped, as they have been in the past, by differential opportunities for employment and higher wages, by largely self-perpetuating social networks that lower the cost of emigration from sending communities, and by political conditions that generate refugee movements.

Finally, some analyses emphasize indirect effects, in which demographic forces have their impacts via intermediary elements. These include the effects of high or low fertility upon age composition (discussed in chapter 2). Rising agrarian population densities may lead to overgrazing and related environmental degradations that may cause outmigration from rural areas. Large cohorts of young adults concentrating in urban areas with high unemployment rates may produce political instabilities, which in turn may result in substantial movements of people.

Like economic theories of international migration, these perspectives drawn from demography offer valuable but only partial explanations, and ultimately they fail to account for many observed patterns of migration. For example, demography-based hypotheses fail to explain the fact that at least until 1990[3] most international migration was *within* the developing world, between countries with similarly high fertility rates and youthful age structures, and that substantial migrations have taken place from very low-fertility Eastern Europe to moderately low-fertility Western Europe, North America, and Australia.

Sociological and Related Theories

Most of the economic and demographic explanations described above lay emphasis upon the forces that affect the *potential* for international migratory movements. With the exception of the "dual labor market" theory, there is but little attention paid to the *actualization* of such potential and to its subsequent persistence. Actualization of potential is discussed below under the Role of the State. The *persistence* of international migration—the fact that migration flows often continue long after the economic and demographic circumstances that underlie them have changed—has been usefully addressed by network and institutional theories arising mainly from sociological analysis.

The *network* theories focus on the transnational social networks that develop between migrants and their kin and neighbors in the origin country. These social connections reduce the risk and lower the costs (economic, psychological, and social) of subsequent migrations, thereby perpetuating and even increasing international migration flows long after the forces that began them have waned.

The *institutional* theories deal with the roles played by intermediaries that emerge to serve the needs of migrants and would-be migrants, discussed in greater detail in the section following.

Recent work to assess the relative importance of demographic and economic differentials and other forces in the enormous wave of migration from Europe during the nineteenth and early twentieth centuries concluded that a combination of economic and demographic differentials and network factors may all have played important roles in explaining the trajectories and pace of the movement of more than 50 million persons who left Europe:

> [R]ates of natural increase at home and income gaps between home and overseas destinations were both important, while industrialization (independent of its influence on real wages) made a moderate contribution. Our results also support the arguments of those who stress the influence of "friends and relatives" among previous emigrants abroad. Our results suggest that these latter effects were strong, creating persistence and path dependence in emigration flows. (Hatton and Williamson 1994: 557)

Intermediaries: International Migration as a Business

The older theories of international migration had a benign quality. There were differential opportunities between countries, of which individuals took advantage to move from one country to another. Countries from which migrants departed benefited from the departure of "surplus" labor that might otherwise be unemployed and perhaps politically explosive; countries that attracted migrants gained their labor and often their entrepreneurial skills. The losses were all short-term, as labor markets equilibrated, societies adjusted to the absorption of people from another culture, and families and individuals endured the pains of cultural loss even as they experienced the exhilaration of building their lives anew.

Yet it is now widely understood that international migration has become an international business—both lawful and unlawful—and a substantial business at that. In the lawful category, one may find in some countries a large cadre of professionals who earn substantial fees in assisting both immigrants and employers. These include:

- *Immigration attorneys*: This has been one of the most rapidly growing elements of the American bar; the American Immigration Lawyers Association now has a membership of over 6,000, and other lawyers also work in this field.
- *Labor recruiters*: This represents an active and profitable service sector in countries such as India, Bangladesh, Pakistan, the Philippines, and Mexico, and is tied in with service providers in the countries of destination.
- *Nonprofit religious and/or humanitarian organizations.*
- *Foreign student recruiters*: Some universities and colleges, seeking fee-paying students, provide substantial payments to student-recruitment firms.
- *Contractors*: In Persian Gulf countries such as Saudi Arabia and Kuwait, foreign firms compete for contracts in construction and services. These companies are often granted permission to recruit and import a specified number of workers to carry out their contracts. In many cases, the governments do not issue visas as such for such workers, but instead so-called "No Objection Certificates" (known as NOC's) which permit labor importation of workers who are authorized to work only for a single employer.

- *Multinational firms*: Large multinationals often recruit globally, on the assumption that they will be able to move their employees from country to country as "intracompany transferees." In countries such as the United States, even small foreign companies with a single office in the United States can qualify for such intracompany transfers.
- *Labor contractors*: These are companies that hire foreign workers and then contract out their services on a daily or hourly basis to other employers. The largest sector here seems to be low-skilled farm workers, such as in California, where labor contractors now dominate the farm labor market. In higher-skill sectors, software service labor contractors have emerged as heavy users of special visas for importation of foreign workers, such as the controversial H-1B visas in the United States.

In the unlawful category, there are now substantial organizations of traffickers, illegal and sometimes predatory organizations of "people-smugglers" that extract large profits from expediting unlawful entry and employment of migrants.[4] According to reports by the International Organization on Migration, this migrant-trafficking activity had already grown into at least a $5 to $7 billion business by the early 1990s (*Migration News* 1994) and has almost certainly increased in size during the late 1990s. Traffickers in Chinese migrants, reportedly based in Taiwan, Hong Kong, Canada, and United States, are known colloquially as "snakeheads." Those smuggling Mexicans and others across the U.S.-Mexico border are called "coyotes." The Russian "mafia" is actively engaged in the transport of Russian and East European women into Western Europe for purposes of prostitution. Other active concentrations of people-smugglers can be found in Haiti, Cuba, Florida, the Bahamas, Morocco, Albania, Mali, and so on.

In Japan, the infamous gangsters known as *yakuza* have for decades been profitably engaged in smuggling Chinese and other nationals into the country. It may be, however, that these *yakuza* people-smuggling activities have created their own competition. Recent accounts suggest that in some criminal activities in Japan, the *yakuza* now are being "driven out by shrewder and more ruthless Chinese gangs." According to one *yakuza*:

> Our biggest problem is the rise of the Chinese mafia. The Chinese gangs are taking business from us in every area—in prostitution, in

gambling, in fencing stolen goods.... The Chinese mafia is very, very good at business. Whether in fake magnetic cards [for pachinko-game arcades] or fencing stolen goods, they go about things with a real system. They are very serious about making money.... For Japanese ya-kuza, the most important thing is staying alive, and making money is second. But for the Chinese gangsters, the first thing is money. The second thing is money. And the third thing is money. (Kristof 1999)

Finally, there is a category of twilight organizations that are engaged in expediting international migration on a sometimes-lawful, sometimes-otherwise basis. These include large numbers of so-called "immigration consultants," some of whom are both competent and law-abiding, some not; and farm labor contractors, legally constituted firms that provide contract workers to farmers with often less-than-careful scrutiny as to their workers' legal status.

The Roles of States: Between the Potential and the Actual

Each of the social science theories outlined above is helpful in increasing our understanding of some of the elements that initiate and perpetuate international migration. A synthetic theory, drawing eclectically upon economic and demographic knowledge, enhanced by an understanding of network and institutional elements, and sensitive to the profit-seeking and rhetorical attractions of migration, offers far better insight into the potential for international migration, and for its subsequent persistence, than do any of these approaches taken separately. Yet even such a synthetic perspective fails to deal adequately with the forces that cause the potential for such migration to be *actualized*.

It is precisely here, at the boundary between the potential and the actual, that the state plays such a central role. The truth is that national governments at the turn of the twenty-first century universally intervene in these flows to influence their size and composition. Yet several commentators have noted that migration theories drawn from the social sciences are strikingly deficient in addressing government action in initiating, selecting, restraining, and ending international migration movements. Zolberg, for example, notes that "it is remarkable that the role of states in shaping international migration has been largely ignored by immigration theorists" (Zolberg 1998).

For some observers, inattention to the role of the state is intentional: They prefer to describe international migration as an inexorable process, driven by hugely powerful economic, demographic, and social forces that overwhelm any efforts by governments to affect them—a kind of human tectonics.[5]

The realities are quite otherwise. Many governments have policies—whether formal or informal, explicit or implicit—that successfully promote the export of migrant labor. There are, likewise, many examples of governmental action (or inaction) that results in mass emigrations due to war, violence, persecution, human rights abuse, mass starvation, and/or ethnic tensions. Finally, of course, all governments have explicit policies to limit inflow or outflow of international migrants.

Migrant-Exporters

It is clear that policies implemented in migrant-sending nations have played a crucial role in shaping levels and patterns of international migration since World War II, yet the attention of theorists has focused almost exclusively on policies within immigrant-receiving societies. Most sending nations have a strong interest in promulgating policies to encourage the international migration of labor. The more obvious examples include the Philippines, Mexico, the Dominican Republic, Bangladesh, India, Turkey, Morocco, Tunisia, El Salvador, Guatemala, Nicaragua, Vietnam, and Barbados, but more muted forms of such policies are practiced in many other countries. The goals are various: to acquire capital, secure foreign exchange, achieve international liquidity, finance trade deficits, relieve unemployment, build skills, or provide a tool of diplomacy.

In the future, it seems likely that more countries will adopt policies that either directly or indirectly favor the emigration of labor, unless their own economies grow rapidly enough to absorb the very large youth-age cohorts that will be reaching labor-force age. Even if relatively few countries do so, it is hard to imagine today's developing countries voluntarily executing policies to prevent emigration from occurring. Indeed, the thrust of recent state policies has been to dismantle barriers to emigration that had existed in many quarters of the world until the early 1980s. In particular, the end of the Cold War, the collapse of the Soviet Union, the democratization of Eastern Europe, and the opening up of China to the global market have combined to reduce political constraints on mobility that, for three decades, had kept world migration from some regions at artificially low levels.

This shift in policy among sending nations has coincided with the rapid expansion of the global economy and the increasing numbers of countries connected to it. As a result, none of the conditions known to play a role in originating international migration—wage differentials, market failures, labor market segmentation, the expansion of global transportation, communications, and social networks—is likely to end anytime soon; and once begun, the forces that perpetuate international movement, as described by social science theory, seem likely to ensure that the resulting migratory flows will persist and expand into the future. Current theoretical and empirical knowledge thus suggests that, in the absence of state interventions, the factors promoting international migration will grow, not decline, throughout the world.

Refugee-Producers

It is also evident that numerous countries engage in practices, or have experienced catastrophes beyond their control, that have the effect of mobilizing large numbers of their citizens to flee in desperation. Consider for example the recent cases of Rwanda, Burundi, Zaire/Congo, Mozambique, Sudan, Somalia, Sierra Leone, Liberia, Myanmar, Afghanistan, Nicaragua, Guatemala, El Salvador, Cuba, Haiti, Bosnia, Croatia, Kosovo, Turkey, Iraq, and Algeria. (This important topic is discussed in greater detail below under the heading entitled "The UN Convention and Protocol on Refugees.")

Universality of State Control on Entry

Finally, all countries (North or South, rich or poor) engage in policies and practices designed to control the number, and/or affect the composition, of migrants crossing their borders. The panoply of policy instruments designed to implement such control is impressive in its ubiquity and scale, comprising both direct controls to prevent unwanted entry, and indirect or remote controls to affect behavior well beyond national borders. They include:

- police controls at borders and ports of entry;
- the now-ubiquitous system of passports and visas, which less than a century ago was a radical innovation;

- sanctions upon international passenger carriers who fail to take due care in transporting passengers lacking required documents;
- collection of intelligence regarding migrant traffickers;
- screening (both internal and external) and adjudication of refugee claimants;
- bilateral and multilateral treaties;
- and policies pursued indirectly via diplomatic, economic, or military actions.[6]

With two types of exception, no sovereign government has ever renounced its right, under the global system of states, to deploy such measures to control the entry of non-nationals across its borders. The exceptions are first, international agreements such as the UN Convention and Protocol regarding refugees, which constrain states from returning refugees to persecution, and second, specific bilateral or multilateral treaties such as those on which the European Union is based.

The UN Convention and Protocol on Refugees The humanitarian disasters of World War II also produced one of the humanitarian achievements of modern history: the international system that provides protection for refugees. Although there had been some ad hoc arrangements, organizations, and international law dealing with this issue, these had failed miserably during the 1930s and 1940s, and in 1951 the still-young United Nations adopted a formal Convention Relating to the Status of Refugees to address the fundamental weakness of international law that had become so apparent (Marrus 1985).

The basic problem was that the existing world system of sovereign states assumed that each person was a citizen of some state, and could call upon it for protection and succor. Yet it was precisely these states that had so flagrantly persecuted their own citizens. At that time, no one was willing to challenge the state's sovereignty over its citizens so long as they remained within their states' boundaries; but what responsibilities did other states have for those who found a way to escape their persecutors by crossing international borders?

The 1951 UN Convention defined as "refugees" a special category of persecuted people who had departed their own states and could not call upon them for protection, and laid down obligations upon other states to admit and protect such people. In the (unfortunately fractured) language of the Convention, a refugee

is a person who, "owing to a well-founded fear of being persecuted for reasons of race, religion, nationality, membership in a
particular social group, or political opinion is outside the country
of his nationality, and is unable or ... unwilling to avail himself
of the protection of that country...."

Hence in international law and international relations, the
term "refugee" has a clear meaning that was carefully crafted.
Signatory states made it very clear that they did not accept any
responsibility to protect citizens of other states, no matter how
desperate their circumstances, unless the other states were themselves practicing "persecution." Moreover, the Convention was
also limited geographically, to the region of Europe which had
produced millions of refugees and displaced persons over the
preceding two decades (Kulischer 1948).

Yet the use of the common English word "refugee" for this
specific category of person has led to enormous confusion and
contention, since the same English word is commonly used by
journalists to refer to persons fleeing natural catastrophes ("the
refugees from the flood"), civil war, generalized violence, environmental degradation, famine, epidemic, poverty, and other circumstances that have nothing to do with "persecution" on the
five grounds specified in the Convention.

In addition, human rights advocates, churches, and political
and ethnic activists objected to these the restrictions embodied in
the UN Convention definition, and in 1967 succeeded in having
the geographical limitation to Europe eliminated in the UN Protocol Relating to the Status of Refugees (Teitelbaum and Russell
1994). But their persistent efforts to expand the core definition of
"refugee" largely failed, with two regional exceptions. In 1969, the
Organization for African Unity (OAU) adopted its own convention with a broader definition of "refugee": "The term refugee
shall also apply to every person who, owing to external aggression, occupation, foreign domination or events seriously disturbing the public order ... is compelled to leave ... to seek refuge in
another place" (Teitelbaum and Russell 1994). Much later, similar
expanded language was incorporated into the Cartegena Declaration relating to the small but strife-torn region of Central America.

There is a final set of definitions and distinctions that have
proved to be important. The UN Convention and Protocol include
a "non-refoulement" provision that prohibits signatory states from
returning *bona fide* refugees to their country of nationality, since
they might be subjected to "persecution." Of course, to qualify as

a "Convention refugee" in the first place, a person must be "outside the country of his nationality." A country sharing a border with another from which refugees are departing due to persecution is therefore obliged not to return them back across this border to continuing persecution, but no signatory state bears any obligation to admit such refugees who have found protection in a country other than their own. This leads to a distinction between "refugees" and "asylum-seekers": to simplify only slightly, asylum-seekers are those who are seeking refugee status not from a place of temporary refuge in a country to which they have initially fled, but instead at or within the borders of another country in which they seek to settle. Thus the distinction between "refugees" and "asylum-seekers" relates mainly to the geographical location of the applicant. A signatory state has an obligation to admit and not return a refugee arriving from a state that is guilty of persecution, but has no obligation to admit equally qualified refugees who have been admitted to other states that are not persecuting them. By the early 1990s, this apparently minor distinction had brought the international refugee system to its deepest crisis since 1951.[7]

Bilateral and Multilateral Treaties   As to bilateral and multilateral cooperation on migration issues, there has been much developed in these domains in just the past decade. In Europe alone, a number of new international instruments have been developed, including the 1990–91 Dublin Convention;[8] the 1990 Schengen Agreement;[9] and the 1992 Edinburgh Declaration. Bilateral agreements have also been signed and ratified, including "readmission agreements" between the United States and Haiti for return of Haitian nationals, and agreements between Germany and its eastern neighbors that embody the "safe third country" concept, that is, transit countries to which asylum-claimants can be returned without violation of the non-refoulement provisions.

Existing security arrangements, developed for reasons other than migration concerns, have also been used to minimize migrations perceived to be destabilizing. NATO and the Organization on Security and Cooperation in Europe (OSCE) have been deeply engaged since 1992 in the political and security implications of asylum, refugee, and migration issues (Russell 1993: 23, 81). The military interventions by NATO in Bosnia and Kosovo were motivated by security threats perceived by NATO member states, conventionally characterized as relevant both to regional stability (from feared violent consequences of ethnic dissolution in Yugoslavia) and to the direct consequences for NATO states of the mass migrations unleashed by violence in these areas. There was, in addition, a more symbolic aspect of NATO concern, in which Bosnia and Kosovo might represent feared harbingers of things to come in NATO countries that are increasingly multicultural, multi-ethnic, and multi-religious. In this view, the West has strong security interests in what happens in these regions of the former Yugoslavia, given that the wars among Serbs, Croats, Bosnian Muslims, and Kosovo Albanians have origins that are deeply cultural, ethnic, and religious. One articulate expression of this concern appeared in the following commentary from *The New Yorker* magazine in 1994:

> Forgetfulness [about Bosnia] would be catastrophic, since Bosnia really does matter to the security of Europe, and the security of Europe, for all the Clinton Administration's efforts to place stronger emphasis on other parts of the world, really does matter to the United States. If the war spills over the borders of Bosnia, Europeans had better learn to duck. But, even if NATO now succeeds in containing the war, the stakes are very high. Bosnia is more than simply another state, internationally recognized in the usual ways. It is a secular state and a democratic one, and it is multicultural, multi-ethnic, and multi-confessional on a continent that, thanks to patterns of migration, is increasingly all those things. If Bosnia's dismemberment is tolerated, nationalist demagogues, in Europe and elsewhere, will take note. (*The New Yorker*, "This is War," 21 February 1994, p. 6)

In the Americas, Costa Rica and Mexico led regional efforts to end the civil wars in Central America so as to minimize the outflow of Central Americans into their countries. The United States, driven largely by concerns about uncontrolled migration, sought first to engage the Organization of American States and subregional Caribbean organizations, but when these efforts failed intervened militarily to reestablish the elected government of Jean-Bertrand Aristide in Haiti.

In Africa, many states have sought to mobilize the Organisation of African Unity to support military action in Somalia, Rwanda, and Zaire/Congo, with concerns about the humanitarian and security implications of mass migrations never far from the surface. The Economic Organization of West African States (ECOWAS) did agree to mobilize military interventions by some of its member states to contain the refugee-producing disorder in Liberia and Sierra Leone. As may be seen from these examples, some efforts by states to reach bilateral or multilateral security agreements on migration issues have met with considerable success, while others may be judged failures. Whether successful or not, all illustrate the growing intersection between migration and security concerns.

To be sure, many efforts by states to exercise control (whether unilateral, bilateral, or multilateral) have attracted controversy and criticism.[10] Much of such criticism is based upon principled opposition to any limitations upon the rights of individuals to claim asylum, as a matter of basic human rights. Other critics act for a variety of less principled motives: ethnic solidarity; political gain; and financial rewards.

Humanitarian military interventions such as those in Somalia, Liberia, Haiti, Bosnia, and Kosovo have also been condemned. Some see them as a new form of neocolonialism; others oppose military intervention on principle; others believe that the circumstances of such cases do not warrant the costs in casualties and expenditures resulting from such intervention.[11]

Likely Trends

While many developing countries can be expected to embrace policies designed to facilitate the departure of their nationals, current theoretical and substantive knowledge portends a growing trend toward more restrictive immigration policies in developed nations, with some though not all receiving nations employing increasingly energetic measures to hinder the entry of uninvited or irregular immigrants, discourage their long-term settlement, and promote their return. Globalization and technological change have contributed to rising international differentials in income, unemployment, or both. They also have served to increase both the absolute and relative number of people seeking to enter as immigrants. Both of these conditions are known theoretically and substantively to push receiving country governments toward restraining immigration. The shift toward such policy regimes is accentuated by the end of the Cold War, which has removed a major ideological prop for expansive immigration policies in Western democracies.

Variable Effectiveness

The ability of states to regulate the behavior of immigrants and control the volume and composition of the resulting flows is constrained, however, by a variety of important influences. Globalization itself limits the power and influence of states to control the transnational movement of labor as well as capital, goods, and information. Likewise the emergence of an international regime protecting human rights constrains the ability of the state and political leaders to respond to the racial and ethnic concerns of voters, or to impose harshly restrictive measures on immigrants or their dependents. These constraints are particularly salient in nations with well-established constitutional protections for individual rights and strong, independent judiciaries.

Thus, having stated that no sovereign state has ever renounced its right to control entry, it must be added that there is great variation over time and place in the effectiveness with which states have exercised this right. Ultimately, the ability of immigrant-receiving states successfully to impose restrictive immigration policies is likely to depend on at least six basic factors:

- the size of the potential flow, both in absolute terms and relative to population size and natural increase;
- the degree of centralized power and relative efficiency of the national bureaucracy;
- the extent to which individual rights are constitutionally protected;
- the relative strength and independence of the judiciary;
- the existence and strength of a historical tradition of immigration; and
- the degree to which a political system is more responsive either to popular opinion or organized interest groups.

The interplay of these factors yields a continuum of state efficacy in restricting immigration. Since many of these instruments represent sometimes controversial intrusions by the state, authoritarian or totalitarian governments often have the most effective policies. At one extreme are nations such as the Gulf States, which counter a moderate demand for entry with powerful centralized bureaucracies, few constitutional protections for individual rights, weak and dependent judiciaries, and no historical traditions of allowing immigration for permanent settlement. Among liberal democratic states, there is tremendous variation in efficacy, emanating from variables such as history, politics, political structure, and geography. Toward the inefficient extreme of the continuum are nations that face a strong demand for entry with relatively weak and decentralized bureaucracies, strong constitutional protections for individual rights, including those of foreigners; a strong and independent judiciary; a long historical tradition of immigration; and a set of politically influential groups with an active interest in immigration questions. Among the least effectual is the United States, with its thousands of miles of land borders and contiguity to numerous island nations with far lower standards of living. Other liberal democracies such as Australia are more effective, aided by geographical location and lack of land borders requiring control.

Yet even for the United States, there can be no real doubt that the magnitudes of immigration are far lower than they would be in the absence of state intervention. A simple but powerful test of this proposition can be found in the case of Puerto Rico. In the absence of state intervention, a far larger proportion of that Caribbean island's population (who are U.S. citizens and hence can move without limitation to anywhere in the United States) is resident in the U.S. mainland than that of any other Caribbean island, notwithstanding the fact that Puerto Rico is by far the most prosperous.

Virtually no systematic research exists to measure exactly how successful countries at different points along this continuum of state efficacy can expect to be as they attempt to limit and control immigration over the next century. Scattered evidence suggests that undocumented (or illegal, or unlawful, or irregular) migration is not unknown even in the Gulf States and is growing throughout Europe and Asia. In the United States, the country for which the data are clearest, both legal and illegal migration continue to expand in spite of recent measures intended to restrict them. It may be that these U.S. policies were designed more as symbolic political gestures, signaling to anxious citizens and workers that their concerns are being addressed, while marginalizing immigrants socially and geographically to make them less visible. What remains to be seen (and better researched) is whether the majority of countries that lie between North America and the Persian Gulf in state capacity will be able to regulate and control immigration over the next century.

Overall, control by states over entry by non-nationals may fairly be described as normal, substantial, and relatively effective—with the latter varying widely. All governments consider such control fundamental to their sovereignty. While many governments are less effective than others in implementing such policies, none will acknowledge that it cannot control such entries, presumably out of fear that such an admission would be politically damaging. In short, claims that increasing potentials for international migration are so powerful that states cannot affect them seem greatly overstated. We can surely acknowledge that a good deal of present-day migration is unwanted by the governments of receiving states, and often in violation of their laws. Still, there is far less international migration occurring than would be the case if states were not regulating entry. Theory-based claims to the contrary ignore much of the reality of the situation.

The powerful impact of states, and the variation in their effectiveness, is discussed usefully in a recent study by a leading French analyst, Patrick Weil. Weil compares the policy behaviors and their impacts of Germany, France, the U.K. and the U.S., and concludes as follows:

> The recent evolution of immigration policies demonstrates the adaptability of the democratic developed States. In reaction to increased migration pressure and the extension of rights for migrants, States have answered by mobilizing more legal, financial and bureaucratic means. Therefore the transformation of migration into a worldwide phenomenon has not automatically involved an increase in immigration flows: when this has happened, it was due primarily to legal windows still open to entry. The closure of these windows has demonstrated that regulation is possible for a democratic state. When the level of uncontrolled flows is still high, as in the United States, it depends more on cultural and historical than on economic or demographic factors. (Weil 1998: 18)

What might be said as to the future stability and security of states, if levels of international migration were to stay high or increase in future years? Might such movements produce significant threats to the internal coherence and stability of receiving states, as the compositions of their populations are rapidly transformed?

Few generalizations are credible here. A wide range of consequences are possible, depending on other forces in the domains of demography, economics, social structure, politics, history, values, and cultures. Not only do factors vary widely from country to country, but in most cases their evolution is almost impossible to predict. The rate of demographic change from both migration and fertility trends may indeed affect political responses. Yet even demographic change can scarcely be anticipated: Will the preferred destinations of today remain constant or change over time? How will fertility rates among natives and migrants evolve? Will there be substantial intermarriage between resident and migrant groups? What current categories of ethnic identity will persist, and which will change?[12]

In this domain, perceptions matter, and matter profoundly. How will the demographic changes that take place be perceived by the public? If, for example, immigrant groups concentrate in a few locations, those already living in these places will perceive the changes in a magnified way, while those in other locations may be unaware of them.

If the society into which migration is occurring is itself experiencing rapid demographic growth due to high rates of natural increase (the difference between births and deaths), the perceived demographic impact of migration may be less than similar volumes of migration into a society experiencing slow indigenous demographic growth. If migrants are considered to be co-ethnics or otherwise similar to the resident population, perceptions of demographic change may be less than with comparable numbers of migrants seen as more distant in ethnic, racial, or linguistic terms.

Finally, if the destination society is troubled by questions of "national identity"—language, history, political systems, art, religion, and so forth—the arrival of foreign migrants can be seen as a threat to the cohesiveness and integration of the society, especially if the number of migrants is increasing rapidly, if their places of settlement are concentrated geographically, or both.

Such concerns did indeed begin to appear in France, Germany, and Quebec during the 1980s. Political parties emerged promising to "protect our national identity against foreigners"—the National Front in France, the Republikaners and similar groups in Germany, the Freedom Party in Austria, and the Parti Québecois in Quebec. Although initially dismissed by the main political party leaderships, over time they began to attract significant numbers of political supporters, and ultimately establishment parties in both France and Germany responded by adopting some of their rhetoric. Consider, for example, the analysis offered by Stanley Hoffmann of the French political scene as of 1994:

> [Premier Edouard Balladur] knows that the National Front's progress, both in percentage of the electorate (12.5 percent in 1993 as against 8.5 in 1988) and in all the traditionally conservative sectors in French society—particularly the rural districts and in the urban lower middle and even upper-middle classes—is a major threat to his own

moderate right constituency. With the enthusiastic help of Interior Minister Pasqua, he has proceeded to appease right-wing voters and impatient deputies with tougher laws on immigration and on the requirements for French nationality....

.... As a clever Machiavellian, Balladur, without making any fundamental changes in French practice, may have pacified the fears of the voters who supported him that French national identity is being eroded. (Hoffmann 1994: 14)

In Austria in early 2000, the Freedom Party led by Jörg Haider, having come in second in the national elections with 27 percent of the vote, succeeded in entering into a governing coalition with the Peoples' Party of Austria. One of the most visible foci of the Freedom Party's platform was upon alleged negative impacts of immigration in Austria. In addition, Haider himself had gained notoriety for past statements concerning the Holocaust, Nazi labor policies, and the Waffen SS. The prospect of the Freedom Party in government evoked an unprecedented set of diplomatic interventions and threatened interventions by other members of the 15-nation European Union. Such pronouncements were driven in part by real concerns about future actions by the new Austrian government, in part by concerns that the Freedom Party's entry into government might legitimize right-wing nationalist parties in other EU countries (especially given the scandals plaguing the Christian Democratic Party in Germany.)

If the perceptions and politics surrounding such issues are unpredictable, so too are economic trends that clearly can affect migration trends and responses to them. Will prosperity increase, and be broadly distributed? Will labor markets be tight or loose? Will unemployment be low or high? Elaborate and sophisticated econometric models have been designed to provide forward looks at economic change, yet the performance record of these models suggests they should be taken seriously only over the short term of years, rather than the decades and generations that are relevant for changes of a demographic, ethnic, social, cultural, and political character.

Given these deep uncertainties, a genuine theory of migration—a set of testable hypotheses that can be rejected by empirical evidence—may well be unattainable. The central roles played by states in affecting the scale and character of migration means that such a theory would require us to know the unknowable: how people of diverse countries, and their governments, will respond to future experiences with international migration.

Notes

1. The study was conducted by a committee of experts convened by the International Union for the Scientific Study of Population (IUSSP); its results were published in a series of journal articles, including Massey et al. (1993: 431–466; 1994: 699–751). For a lucid summary, see Russell (1995).
2. See, for example, Wattenberg (1987). For a hypothetical simulation of the magnitudes of immigration that would be required to hold constant the ratio of over-60 to working-age populations, see United Nations (2000).
3. The latest revision of the UN report indicates that since 1990 there has been a trend toward migration from developing to developed countries. See United Nations (2000).
4. These range from the inexpensive smuggling services along the Mexico-U.S. border to the $30,000–$40,000 per person services provided to mainland Chinese by the organized crime syndicates known as Triads.
5. For examples of this approach, see Cornelius, Martin, and Hollifield (1994).
6. For a fuller discussion, see Teitelbaum (2001).
7. For a more detailed discussion, see Teitelbaum and Winter (1998).
8. The Dublin Convention is more formally known as the "Convention Determining the State Responsible for Examining Applications for Asylum Lodged in One of the Member States of the European Communities." It was signed by the 12 member states in 1990 and 1991. For a fuller discussion, see Hovy and Zlotnik (1994) and Russell, Keely, and Christian (2000).
9. The Schengen Agreement is among Belgium, France, Germany, Luxembourg, the Netherlands, Italy, Spain, and Portugal.
10. For a discussion, see Teitelbaum (2001).
11. The Washington Post invoked all of these arguments in a June 1994 editorial, "Invade Haiti?," opposing military intervention in Haiti.
12. For a sophisticated discussion of these uncertainties as they affect long-range demographic projections, see Smith and Edmonston (1997).

— *Nine* —

INTERNATIONAL MIGRATION AS A SECURITY THREAT?

———ண———

With the end of the Cold War, the notion of "security" has taken on an entirely new dimension. Both states and regimes can be made insecure by factors other than the threat of armed attack, and among these is clearly an unwanted population influx. Migration and refugee issues, no longer the sole concern of ministries of labor or immigration, are now matters of high international politics, engaging the attention of heads of state, cabinets, and key ministries involved in defense, internal security, and external relations. One of the most dramatic high-politics events involving international migration was the exodus of East Germans to Austria through Czechoslovakia and Hungary in July and August of 1989. This exodus precipitated the decision of the German Democratic Republic to open its western borders, resulting in a massive migration westward followed by the fall of the East German government, and the absorption of East Germany by the Federal Republic of Germany. It was flight, not invasion, that ultimately destroyed the East German state.

The hopes of millions of migrants and refugees for a better life and freedom from violence and repression are matched by the fears of many governments and their citizens that a massive influx of newcomers will impose strains on the economy, upset a precarious ethnic balance, weaken the national identity, or threaten political upheaval. This chapter provides a summary of the variety of ways in which migrants and refugees are perceived as potential threats to the security of states or regimes. Examples abound in the mass media of migration flows that have generated conflicts within and between states and have therefore risen to the top of the political agenda, and from which one may make three points.

First, as discussed in chapters 6 to 8, international migration shows no sign of abating. Indeed, the end of the Cold War has precipitated a resurgence of violent attempts at both secession and "ethnic cleansing," both of which have created sometimes massive refugee flows. The breakup of empires and countries into smaller units has created minorities who now feel insecure, and majority populations who in some cases seek to magnify such insecurity so as to encourage their departure. Vast differentials in income and employment opportunities among countries persist, providing the push and pull that motivate economic migrants. Environmental degradation, droughts, floods, famines, and civil conflicts compel people to flee across international borders, while new global networks of communication and transportation provide individuals with information and opportunities for migration.

Second, more people want to leave their countries than other countries are willing or able to accept. The reluctance of states to open their borders to all who wish to enter is only partly a concern over economic effects. The constraints are as likely to be political, resulting from concern that an influx of people belonging to another ethnic community may generate xenophobic sentiments, incite conflicts between natives and migrants, and spur the growth of anti-migrant right-wing parties.

Third, there are real concerns, in many world regions, that massive flows of refugees offer attractive settings through which aggressive states and non-state actors may "place" their operatives in sensitive locations abroad. Such concerns have long been prominent in Pakistan, in Zaire/Congo, and in the Balkans, but have more recently come to the fore with the apprehension of alleged Islamic terrorists carrying explosive materials who were seeking to enter the United States after having established legal residence in Canada.

It is necessary to note that only a fraction of the world's 14.1 million refugees and asylum-seekers, and more than 21 million internally displaced persons (as of December 31, 1999) are in the advanced industrial countries (U.S. Committee for Refugees 2000:

Tables 2 and 5). Moreover, only a small though perhaps increasing portion of global migration has flowed to European OECD countries, where the (reported) foreign or foreign-born population ranges from less than 2 percent in Spain, Portugal, Greece, and Finland, to nearly 20 percent in Switzerland and 34 percent in Luxembourg. In the larger countries in this group, the percentages were 6 and 9 percent in France and Germany respectively (OECD 1998: Table 1.3). Most human migratory movements have been from one developing country to another: The world's largest refugee flows have been in Africa, South Asia, Southeast Asia, and in the Persian Gulf.

Surprisingly little systematic comparative attention has been given to the ways in which international population movements create conflicts within and between states. A study of these effects is necessary to understand why states and their citizens often have an aversion to international migration even when it is accompanied by economic benefits.

Economic factors (as discussed in chapter 7) go a long way toward explaining a great many international population movements, but they neglect two critical political elements. The first is that international population movements are often impelled, encouraged, or prevented by governments or political forces for reasons that may have little to do with economic conditions. Indeed, many international population flows, especially within Africa and South Asia, are only marginally, if at all, determined by changes in the global or regional political economy. And secondly, even when economic conditions create inducements for people to leave one country for another, it is governments that decide whether their citizens should be allowed or encouraged to leave and governments that decide whether immigrants should be allowed or encouraged to enter, and these governmental decisions are frequently based on non-economic considerations. Moreover, governments vary in their capacity to control entry. States that are capable of defending themselves against missile, tank, and infantry attacks are often unable to defend themselves against the intrusion of thousands of illegal immigrants crossing a border in search of employment or safety. Yet governments generally want to control the entry of people, and regard their inability to do so as a threat to sovereignty. Any effort, therefore, to develop a framework for the analysis of transnational flows of people must also take into account the political determinants and constraints upon these flows.

A security/stability framework complements rather than replaces an economic analysis by focusing upon the role of states in both creating and responding to international migration. This framework may be constructed in three ways: First, by identifying types of international movements generated by considerations of state security and stability, as distinct from those flows largely shaped by the regional or international political economy. Such movements include forced and induced emigrations as examples of politically driven population movements with international repercussions. Second, by describing those circumstances in which international migration is regarded as a threat to a country's security and stability. This leads us to consider how and when refugees and economic migrants come to be regarded as threatening by receiving and sending countries. And finally, by considering the various ways states react when faced with population movements they regard as a threat to their international security and internal stability.

Forced and Induced Emigration: A Global Perspective

It would be inaccurate to assume that much of the world's population flows merely happen; more often they are made to happen. There are three distinct types of forced and induced emigrations in the contemporary world.

First, governments may force emigration as a means of achieving cultural homogeneity or asserting the dominance of one ethnic community over another. Such flows have a long and sordid history. Accompanying the rise of nationalism in Europe were state actions to eject religious communities that did not subscribe to the established religion and ethnic minorities that did not belong to the dominant ethnic community. In the fifteenth century the Spanish crown exiled the Jews; in the seventeenth and eighteenth centuries, the British crown induced Protestant dissenters to settle in the American colonies; and in the early decades of the twentieth century, minorities throughout Eastern Europe—Bulgarians, Greeks, Jews, Turks, Hungarians, Serbs, and Macedonians—were put to flight (Kulischer 1948: 248–249).

Contemporary population movements in post-colonial Africa, the Middle East, South Asia, and Southeast Asia are similarly linked to the rise of nationalism and the emergence of new states. The boundaries of many of the new post-colonial regimes divided linguistic, religious, and tribal communities, with the result that minorities, fearful for their future and often faced with discrimination and violence, migrated to join their ethnic brethren in a neighboring country.

Many Third World countries also expelled their ethnic minorities, especially when the minorities constituted an industrious class of migrant origin in competition with a middle-class ethnic majority. Governments facing unemployment within the majority community and conflicts among ethnic groups over language and educational opportunities often regarded the expulsion of a prosperous, well-placed minority as a politically popular policy. Economically successful minorities have often been told that others would be given preference in employment, a policy of discrimination that effectively makes it difficult for minorities to compete on the basis of merit. The list of expulsions is long, with notable examples in only the past decades including Indians and Pakistanis from Uganda, Kurds from Turkey and Iraq, and Tutsis from Rwanda. To this list from the Third World, we must now add the minorities in each of the successor states of Yugoslavia.

Secondly, governments have forced emigration as a means of dealing with political dissidents and class enemies. The ancient Greeks were among the earliest to strip dissidents of citizenship and cast them into exile. Socrates himself was offered the option of going into exile rather than being executed. Contemporary authoritarian governments have expelled dissidents or allowed them to go into exile as an alternative to imprisonment. Exiles in the United States from the Third World have largely replaced exiles from Europe.

Governments may expel not just a handful of dissidents, but a substantial portion of the population hostile to the regime. Revolutionary regimes often see large-scale emigration of an entire social class as a way of transforming the country's social structure. The exodus of more than a half million members of the Cuban middle class was regarded by the Castro regime as a way of disposing of a social class hostile to socialism. For different reasons, the Duvalier regime of Haiti took similar action against the Haitian middle class.

A third type of forced migration can be described as part of a strategy to achieve a foreign policy objective. Although they may deny such an intent, governments may, for example, force emigration as a way of putting pressure on neighboring states. The refugee-receiving country often understands that a halt to unwanted migration is not likely to take place unless it yields on a demand made by the country from which the refugees come. In 1981, for example, the U.S. government believed that the government of Haiti was encouraging its citizens to flee by boat to Florida to press the United States to substantially increase its economic aid. Whether the emigration represented Haitian policy or not, the United States did increase aid to Haiti.

Colonization long served as a means for imperial powers to extend their political or economic dominance, while decolonization has provided an opportunity for successor regimes to consolidate the power and position of their own ethnic groups. During the colonial expansions of the eighteenth and nineteenth centuries, the imperial powers moved populations from one territory to another in pursuit of their own economic interests. Slaves were transported from Africa to the Caribbean and to North America. After the abolition of slavery, the British established a system of indentured labor that enabled them to satisfy the labor needs in their colonies (especially on British-owned plantations) by moving Indians to East Africa, Mauritius, the Caribbean, Fiji, and Sri Lanka. The colonial powers also encouraged the migration of entrepreneurial communities, traders, and money lenders whom they regarded as politically pliable, for example, Indians to the Gulf States, Lebanese to West Africa, and Chinese to Southeast Asia.

While the colonization of distant territories rarely led to enduring political or economic control, the colonization of nearby territories has almost always had permanent consequences. Americans moved westward into Mexican and Native American territories; the Chinese colonized non-Han areas. These flows displaced the local populations and transformed the politics of the areas that were colonized.

Colonization as a means of international conquest and annexation can in fact be the deliberate intent of a state. The government of Morocco, for example, moved 350,000 civilians into Western Sahara in an effort to claim and occupy disputed territory. The Israeli government provided housing subsidies to its citizens to settle in the West Bank. Since the annexation of the Turkic regions of Central Asia in the nineteenth century the czarist and Soviet regimes encouraged Russian settlement, while a similar policy of settling Han people has been pursued by the Chinese government in Sinkiang province and Tibet.

Upon independence from European colonialism, many newly established regimes sought to "decolonize" themselves by pressing for the exodus of populations they regarded as imposed upon them by the imperial power. With few exceptions, white settlers were pressed to return home. French settlers vacated Algeria; most Portuguese left Angola and Mozambique; many British left Zimbabwe. The new regimes often pressed for the exodus of those who had been brought in by the imperial rulers as indentured servants, although they were now free laborers and many had become prosperous businessmen and members of the middle class. Sri Lanka pressed for the departure of Tamil tea estate workers. A similar process of rejection may someday be at work in the former Soviet republics, where millions of Russian "colons" are regarded as illegitimate settlers imposed by the Soviet regime (Brubaker 1993).

Forced emigration can be an instrument by which one state seeks to destabilize another, force recognition, stop a neighboring state from interfering in its internal affairs, prod a neighboring state to provide aid or credit in return for stopping the flow, or extend its own political and economic interests or those of a dominant ethnic group through colonization or decolonization. An examination of both historical and contemporary population movements thus demonstrates that countries of emigration have more control over international population flows than is usually accounted for by political analysts, and that what often appear to be spontaneous emigration and refugee movements may represent deliberate emigration policies on the part of sending countries. To view refugee flows as simply the unintended consequences of internal upheavals or economic crises is to ignore the eagerness of some governments to reduce or eliminate selected social classes and ethnic groups from within their own borders and to affect the politics and policies of their neighbors.

Migration as a Threat to Security and Stability

Migration can be perceived as threatening by governments of either population-sending or population-receiving communities. Armed refugees may pose the threat of attack; migrants can be a threat to either country's political stability; or migrants may be perceived as a threat to the major societal values of the receiving country.

"Security" is a social construct with different meanings in different societies. An ethnically homogeneous society, for example, may place higher value on preserving its ethnic character than does a heterogeneous society and may, therefore, regard a population influx as a threat to its security. Providing a haven for those who share one's values (political freedom, for example) is important in some countries, but not in others. In some countries, therefore, an influx of "freedom fighters" may not be regarded as a security threat. Moreover, even in a given country opinions as to what is highly valued may not be shared equally by elites and counter-elites. The influx of migrants regarded as radicals may be feared by a monarch, but welcomed by the opposition. One ethnic group may welcome migrants, while another is vehemently opposed to them. The business community may be more willing than the general public to import migrant workers.

Similarly, countries differ in whether or not they regard the mistreatment of their citizens abroad as a threat that calls for state action. While some countries are prepared to take armed action in defense of their overseas citizens, others prefer not to antagonize a government that has enabled its citizens to find employment and earn much-needed remittances.

One can identify five broad situational categories in which refugees or migrants may be perceived as a threat to the country that produces the emigrants, to the country that receives them, or to relations between sending and receiving countries. The first is when refugees and migrants are regarded as a threat—or at least an irritant—in relations between sending and receiving countries, a situation that often arises when refugees and migrants are opposed to the regime of their home country. The second is when migrants or refugees are perceived as a political threat or security risk to the regime of the host country. The third is when immigrants are seen as a cultural threat or, fourth, as a social and economic problem for the host society. And the fifth—a new element growing out of developments in the Persian Gulf—is when the host society uses immigrants as an instrument of threat against the country of origin. We discuss each of these in turn.

Refugees and Immigrants as Opponents of Their Home Regime Conflicts create refugees, but refugees can also create conflicts. Such an international conflict can arise when a country classifies individuals as refugees with a well-founded fear of persecution, thereby accusing and condemning the country of origin for engaging in persecution. The mere granting of asylum can create an antagonistic relationship. Thus, the January 1990 debate in Congress over whether Chinese students should be permitted to remain in the United States because of persecution in China was regarded by the People's Republic of China as "interference" in its internal affairs. President Bush was prepared to permit graduating students and other Chinese in the United States to remain by extending their visas, but not to grant asylum, while many in Congress wanted to grant formal asylum status in order to condemn China.

To the chagrin of migrant-producing countries, democratic regimes generally allow refugees to speak out against the regime of their country of origin, allow them access to the media, and permit them to send information and money back home in support of the opposition. The host country's decision to grant refugee status thus often creates an adversarial relationship with the country that produces the refugees. The receiving country may have no such intent, but even when its motives are humanitarian, the mere granting of asylum can be sufficient to create an antagonistic relationship. In perhaps the most famous asylum episode of the past century, Iranian revolutionaries took violent exception to the U.S. decision to permit the Shah of Iran to enter the United States for medical reasons; many Iranians regarded this as a form of asylum, and some used it as an occasion for taking American hostages.

A refugee-receiving country may actively support refugees in their quest to change the regime of their country of origin. Refugees are potentially a tool in interstate conflict: The United States armed *contra* exiles from Nicaragua; the Indian government armed Bengali "freedom fighters" against the Pakistani military; the Chinese provided arms to the Khmer Rouge refugees to help overthrow the Vietnamese-backed regime in Cambodia; and Palestinian refugees received support from Arab countries for their actions against Israel. Therefore, refugee-producing countries may have good reason for fearing an alliance between their adversaries and their expatriates.

Non-refugee immigrants can also be a source of conflict between receiving and sending countries. A diaspora made up primarily of refugees is, of course, likely to be hostile to the regime of the country from which they fled. But even economic migrants may become hostile, especially if they live in democratic countries while the government of their homeland is repressive. Thus, many Chinese lost their sympathy for China's government in 1989, when the regime became repressive at Tiananmen Square. Thereafter, many overseas Chinese supported dissidents within China and pressed their host governments to withdraw support from China. The Beijing government came to regard many overseas Chinese as a source of support for dissidents.

The home country may take a dim view of the activities of its citizens abroad, and hold the host country responsible for their activities. But host countries, especially if they are democratic, are loath to restrict migrants engaged in lawful activities, especially since some of the migrants have already become citizens. Thus, struggles that might otherwise take place only within a country become internationalized if the country has a significant overseas population.

Refugees and Immigrants as a Political Risk to the Host Country Governments are often concerned that refugees to whom they give protection may turn against them if they are unwilling to assist the refugees in their opposition to the government of their country of origin. Paradoxically, the risk may be particularly high if the host country has gone so far as to arm the refugees against their country of origin. Guns can be pointed in both directions, and the receiving country takes the risk that refugees will seek to dictate the host country's policies toward the sending country.

For example, the decision by Arab countries to provide residence, political support, and arms to Palestinian refugees from Israel created a population within the Arab states capable of influencing the foreign policies and internal politics of these states. Palestinians became a political and security problem for Lebanon, Syria, Jordan, Israel, France, and the United States. The support of Iraqi invaders by Palestinians in Kuwait was an asset to Iraq, since some of the 400,000 Palestinians in Kuwait held important positions in the Kuwaiti administration. The Kuwaiti government's decision to expel most Palestinians after the Gulf War reflected its view that this guest population had become a security threat. Throughout the Middle East, governments have had to consider the capacity of resident Palestinians to undermine their regimes should they adopt policies unacceptable to the Palestinians.

Refugees have launched terrorist attacks within their host countries, illegally smuggled arms, allied with the domestic opposition against the host-government policies, participated in drug trafficking, and in other ways eroded governments' willingness to admit refugees. Armenians, Croats, Kurds, Northern Irish, Palestinians, Sikhs, and Sri Lankan Tamils, among others, have been regarded with suspicion by intelligence and police authorities of other countries; their requests for asylum have been scrutinized not only for whether they have a well-founded fear of persecution, but for whether their presence might constitute a threat to the host country.

These fears, it should be noted, are sometimes exaggerated. Governments have often gone to extreme lengths to protect themselves against low-level threats. Yet, these fears are not always unfounded, especially in the context of an increase in international terrorism.

Migrants Perceived as a Threat to Cultural Identity How and why some migrant communities are perceived as cultural threats is a complicated issue, initially involving how the host community defines itself. Cultures differ with respect to how they define who belongs or who can be admitted into their community. Varying norms govern who is admitted, what rights and privileges are given to those who are permitted to enter, and whether the host culture regards a migrant community as potential citizens. A violation of these norms (by unwanted immigrants, for example) is often regarded as a threat to basic values and in that sense is perceived as a threat to national security.

These norms are often embedded in the law of citizenship that determines who, by virtue of birth, is entitled as a matter of right to be a citizen and who is permitted to become a naturalized citizen. The main distinction is between citizenship laws based on *jus sanguinis*—whereby a person wherever born is a citizen of the state of his parents—and those based on *jus soli*—the rule that a child receives his nationality from the soil or place of birth. The ties of blood descent are broader than merely parentage, for they suggest a broader *volk*, or people, to whom one belongs in a fictive relationship. The Federal Republic of Germany, for example, has such a legal norm. Under a law passed in 1913—and only recently modified—German citizenship at birth was based exclusively on descent (*jus sanguinis*); thus the children of migrants born in Germany were not thereby automatically entitled to citizenship (no *jus soli*).

The 1913 law was substantially changed in 1999, after a contentious and hard-fought debate. The question was driven initially by ethnic politics and by broader concerns about Germany's failure to integrate many of its longtime Turkish residents into German society. Ultimately proposed changes to the citizenship law ran afoul of concerns about the implications of dual nationality.

German adherence to *jus sanguinis*, coupled with large-scale immigration that began with the *gastarbeiter* program in the late

1950s, resulted by the late 1990s in a sub-population of hundreds of thousands of children of immigrants who were born and raised in Germany but were not entitled to German nationality. While naturalization was a theoretical possibility for such persons, the law required 15 years of German residency and a complicated and sometimes expensive administrative and legal procedure, and naturalization rates proved to be very low.

During the 1998 national election, most polls reported that immigration was second only to unemployment as a campaign issue, and a 1998 Forsa poll found that 52 percent of German voters thought there were too many foreigners in Germany and an that 10 percent would consider voting for an extreme anti-immigrant political party. With the exception of the Greens, all German parties supported limitations on immigration and the removal of foreign criminals. The Christian Democratic Union and Christian Social Union (CDU/CSU) platform, for example, stated:

> To help keep our nation foreigner-friendly, the integration capacity and the integration willingness of the Germans must not be overtaxed. Therefore, the arrival [of foreigners] must remain as tightly limited as possible. Those who demand immigration for our densely populated country endanger domestic peace. Such people also assist radical forces.... People who want to live long term in Germany must also be prepared to fit in to our society and set of values. They need to adjust to our way of living, respect our laws and our manner of behavior.... Anybody who wants to become a German citizen must be ready to give up their old citizenship. (*Migration News* 1998)

Then-Chancellor Helmut Kohl said that "Germany must not become a land of immigrants [and should remain] a bastion of Christian civilization," while the Social Democratic (SPD) candidate Gerhard Schroeder said that Germany "can no longer bear the burden of hosting a much greater share of immigrants than other European countries." In her farewell press conference in August 1998, the Commission for Foreigners appointed by the CDU/CSU government, Cornelia Schmalz-Jacobsen, criticized the major political parties for making immigration a major campaign issue (*Migration News* 1998).

In the election, the SPD party achieved a plurality of 41 percent of the vote to a CDU/CSU total of 35 percent. Apart from the two major parties, the party that most strongly supported substantial immigration, the Greens, received about 7 percent, while the party most opposed to immigration, the Republikaners, received less than 5 percent. The Free Democrats, the FDP, which had long been part of a governing coalition with the CDU/CSU, got 6 percent, while the former communist party of the East, the PDS, got 5 percent. Given this outcome, the SPD decided to form a coalition government with the Greens, which it described as the "red-green coalition."

Led by the Green Party and Turkish ethnic organizations, this new governing coalition proposed legislative changes that would adopt the *jus soli* principle for children born to foreign nationals lawfully resident in Germany, and would also facilitate naturalization and dual nationality for both foreign-born and German-born "foreigners" under then-current law. Their declared goals were to improve inter-ethnic relations in Germany, especially with respect to the 2.1 million German residents with Turkish nationality.

The government's proposals were that all children born in Germany be automatically entitled to German citizenship, so long as at least one parent was German-born or had entered Germany before age 14 and had a legal residence permit. For those not qualifying under this provision, the number of years required for naturalization would be reduced from 15 to eight years. In both cases, those granted German nationality would be allowed to retain their prior nationality; thus dual citizenship would be legally tolerated if not encouraged. The governing coalition's embrace of dual nationality, in addition to providing eased access to German citizenship by birth and naturalization, was based on the argument that German citizenship would foster the integration of the millions of Turks in Germany, but that many would be reluctant to renounce their Turkish nationality, both for reasons of national/ethnic pride and to preserve their inheritance rights in Turkey (*The Economist* 1999). Opponents argued that the dual nationality provision would promote divided national loyalties. By raising doubts about dual nationals' commitment to Germany, they claimed, it would thereby impede the acceptance and integration of Turks in Germany.

In 1999 a compromise nationality law was adopted under which children born to foreign parents who have lived in Germany for at least eight years will have dual nationality, but between ages 18 and 23 they will have to choose one or the other. Eligibility for naturalization will require eight rather than 15 years of residence. Naturalization will require applicants to speak

German, not to have been convicted of criminal activities resulting in prison terms exceeding nine months, not to be dependent
on government welfare programs, and to sign a statement declar-
ing respect for Germany's constitution. The estimated 450,000
immigrants who have lived in Germany for more than 30 years,
or who are over 60 years of age, will be entitled to claim German
citizenship while retaining their other nationality.[1]

The Basic Law (Germany's postwar "constitution") also ac-
cords citizenship to those Germans who do not live in Germany
and who may not speak German but who came (or are descended
from those who came) from Germany and the territories from
which Germans were expelled after World War II (Hailbronner
1989). Thus, thousands of immigrants who entered the Federal
Republic from East Germany after the war, or from Poland,
Czechoslovakia, Romania, and elsewhere, were regarded as German citizens returning "home." Other countries share a similar
concept. Israel, for example, has a Law of Return under which all
Jews, irrespective of where they presently live, are entitled to
"return" home to reclaim, as it were, their citizenship. Nepal also
has a law that entitles those who are of Nepali origin, though they
and their ancestors have lived in India, Singapore, Hong Kong, or
elsewhere for several generations, to reclaim their citizenship by
returning "home." Somewhat different but related policies are followed in Italy with respect to Italians who emigrated to
Argentina, and in Japan with respect to Japanese-origin citizens of
Latin American countries such as Peru and Brazil.

Where such notions of consanguinity dominate citizenship
law, the political system is attempting to distinguish between an
acceptable and unacceptable influx, without regard either to the
number of immigrants or to the condition of the economy into
which the immigrants move. In general, countries with norms of
consanguinity find it difficult to incorporate ethnically alien
migrants, including refugees, into citizenship. These countries
are also likely to have political groups that advocate sending
immigrants home even though expulsion may impose severe
economic consequences for the host as well as home countries.

A norm of indigenousness may also be widely shared by a section of a country's population and even incorporated into its legal
system. This norm prescribes different rights for those who are
classified as indigenous and those who, irrespective of the length
of time they or their ancestors resided in the country, are not so
classified. An indigenous people asserts a superior claim to land,

employment, education, political power, and central national symbols that is not accorded to others who live within the country. The indigenes may assert exclusive rights denied to others, often resting on the notion that they as a people exist only within one country, while others have other homes to which they can return. Thus, the Sinhalese in Sri Lanka, the Malays (the *bhoomiputras*) in Malaysia, the Assamese in Assam, and the Melanesians in Fiji, among others, subscribe to an ideology of indigenousness that has, in various guises, been enshrined in the legal system and that shapes the response of these societies to immigrants.

Nativism, a variant of the norm of indigenousness, played an important role in shaping the U.S. Immigration Act of 1924, particularly its national origins clause providing for national quotas. This legislation, and the political sentiment that underlay it, resulted in a restrictive policy toward migration throughout the 1930s and early 1940s. After the war, however, the older American tradition of civic pluralism became politically dominant. It shaped the 1965 Immigration Act, which eliminated national quotas and gave preferences to skilled individuals and to family unification. The numbers and composition of migrants then significantly changed. From the mid-1960s to the late 1990s, between 500,000 and 1 million migrants and refugees entered each year, with nearly half the immigrants coming from Asia.

Citizenship in the United States is acquired by birth or by naturalization. Originally, American law permitted naturalization only to "free white persons" but subsequent acts permitted naturalization without regard to race. Apart from the usual residence requirements, U.S. naturalization law requires applicants to demonstrate basic knowledge of the American Constitution and form of government and to swear allegiance to the principles of the Constitution. Political knowledge and loyalty, not consanguinity, are thus the norms for membership. It is in part because the United States has political rather than ethnic criteria for naturalization that the United States has been more supportive of immigrants than most other countries.

For much of France's history, a low-level threat perception has characterized that country's response to immigration. While a concern for cultural unity is a central element in the French conception of nationhood, the French have also had a political conception of citizenship derived from revolutionary origins. The French tradition is universalist and assimilationist, in contrast with the *volk*-centered Germans (Brubaker 1989). The result is that the French have been more willing to naturalize immigrants than have the Germans and have been more open to political refugees than most other West European countries. Even so, France has a strong anti-migrant movement, the National Front, led by Jean-Marie Le Pen, a North African-born Frenchman who has won considerable support for his position that guest workers from North Africa and their French-born children should "return home" to North Africa.

Migrants Perceived as a Social or Economic Burden Societies may react to immigrants because of the economic costs they impose or because of purported social behavior such as criminality, welfare dependency, and delinquency. Societies may be concerned because the people entering are so numerous or so poor that they create a substantial economic burden by straining housing, education, and transportation facilities. In advanced industrial societies, services provided by the welfare state may generate local resentment. In less-developed countries, refugees may illegally occupy private or government lands; their goats, sheep, and cattle may decimate forests and grazing land; they may use firewood, consume water, produce waste, and in other ways come to be regarded as an ecological threat.

The willingness to bear these costs is likely to be low if the host government believes that the government of the sending country is engaged in a policy of population "dumping," by exporting its criminals, unwanted ethnic minorities, and "surplus" population at the cost of the receiving country. The United States, for example, welcomed those Cubans who fled the communist regime in the 1960s but not Cuban convicts removed from prisons and placed on boats bound for the United States in the 1970s. Governments also distinguish between situations in which ethnic minorities are permitted to leave (for example, Jews from the Soviet Union) and those in which minorities are forced to flee (Bulgarian Turks or Sri Lankan Tamils) and are, therefore, more likely to accept the former than the latter.

Population dumping has not been a significant element in the flow of migrants from developing countries to advanced industrial countries. To the extent that population dumping has occurred, it has largely been of ethnic minorities. Such flights, at least before the Yugoslav crisis, have primarily been to neighboring developing countries rather than to advanced industrial countries.

Forced population movements of ethnic minorities took place in Eastern Europe during the interwar period, placing enormous economic and social pressures upon the receiving countries, taking a heavy toll on the migrants themselves, and worsening relations among states. But because there was an element of exchange, and minorities moved to states in which their ethnic community was a majority, settlement was possible and violent international conflict was avoided. In 1922–23, for example, Greeks fled Turkey and Turks fled Greece; an estimated 1.5 million people from both countries were involved. In a related population exchange, in 1923 the Greek government, in an effort to Hellenize its Macedonian region, forced the exodus of its Bulgarian population. As the Bulgarian refugees moved into Greek-speaking areas of Bulgaria, the local Greek population fled southward to Greece (Marrus 1985).

The world's largest population exchange was in South Asia, where 14 million people moved between India and Pakistan between 1947 and 1950. But since both countries respected the wishes of each other's ethnic minorities to settle in the country in which they constituted a majority, the exchange itself did not cause a conflict between the two nations. Similarly, the forced exit of Jews from North Africa to Israel in the 1950s was not a source of international conflict, since the refugees were welcomed. In contrast, however, the flight of Arabs from Israel in 1948 led to an interminable conflict between Israel and its Arab neighbors, since the Arab states did not recognize the legitimacy of the new Israeli state (Morris 1987).

Government officials, otherwise concerned with the plight of refugees, may fear that a decision to grant refugee status to a small number of individuals might open a floodgate and lead to the entry of more immigrants than society is prepared to accept. One reason states hesitate to grant refugee and asylum status to those fleeing because of economic or even violent conditions at home—as distinct from having a personal "well-founded fear of persecution"—is the concern that the number of asylum requests would then increase. States prefer restrictive criteria in order to keep the influx small. Since laws of asylum are always imprecise and the pledge to admit refugees with a well-founded fear of persecution is subject to varied interpretations, individuals who wish to enter a country but cannot do so under existing guest worker and migration laws may resort to claiming political asylum. West European governments are thus torn between a humanitarian sentiment toward refugees and the recognition that the more generous the law of asylum, the greater the number of applicants. As the number of asylum seekers grows, governments become more restrictive, insisting on evidence that the applicant does indeed have a well-founded fear of individual persecution, not "merely" a fear of being killed in a violent civil conflict. A large increase in asylum applications to Switzerland in 1986 and 1987, for example, led to passage of a referendum imposing a ceiling on the number of entries under the laws of asylum.

In recent years Western Europe has become more restrictive as the requests for asylum have increased. At one extreme, some political leaders argue that to admit even a small number of refugees who enter because of political conditions or violence at home would open the door to larger numbers than their societies are prepared to admit. The mainstream consensus, however, increasingly points to reform of asylum adjudication and benefits systems to minimize the improper use of asylum claims by those seeking more promising economic conditions. Numerous measures of this type have been undertaken, especially in countries such as Germany that experience very large numbers of asylum claims. The effects of such measures can be easily discerned in the numbers (see Table 9.1).

The number of asylum claims filed in Germany rose from 57,000 in 1987 to 438,000 in 1992. With the adoption of new asylum procedures in 1993, the number of claims began to recede, and by 1997 it was 104,000—still nearly twice the 1987 number, but a quarter of that in the peak year of 1992. Similar, if less dramatic, patterns and trends can be discerned in other countries such as the United States, Austria, and France.

Migrants as Hostages: Risks for the Sending Country Recent actions of the governments of Iran, Iraq, and Libya all demonstrate how migrants can be used as an instrument of statecraft in order to impose restraints upon the actions of the home government. Following the invasion of Kuwait on August 2, 1990, the government of Iraq announced a series of measures using migrants as instruments for the achievement of political objectives. Iraq declared that Westerners living in Iraq and Kuwait would be forcibly held as a shield against armed attack, in an effort to deter the United States and its allies from launching air strikes against military facilities where hostages might be located. The Iraqi government then indicated its willingness to treat the migrants of those countries that did not send troops to Saudi Arabia, such as India, more favorably than the migrants of those countries that did, such as Pakistan and Bangladesh. The Iraqi government

TABLE 9.1: Inflows of Asylum Seekers into Selected OECD Countries (thousands)

	1987	1988	1989	1990	1991	1992	1993	1994	1995	1996	1997
Australia	::	::	0.5	3.8	17.0	4.1	4.6	4.2	5.1	6.0	7.7
Austria	11.4	15.8	21.9	22.8	27.3	16.2	4.7	5.1	5.9	7.0	6.7
Belgium	6.0	4.5	8.2	13.0	15.4	17.6	26.5	14.7	11.7	12.4	11.6
Canada	35.0	45.0	19.9	36.7	32.3	37.7	21.1	21.7	25.6	25.7	23.9
Czech Republic	::	::	::	1.8	2.0	0.9	2.2	1.2	1.4	2.0	2.1
Denmark	2.7	4.7	4.6	5.3	4.6	13.9	14.3	6.7	5.1	5.9	5.1
Finland	-	0.1	0.2	2.7	2.1	3.6	2.0	0.8	0.8	0.7	1.0
France	27.6	34.3	61.4	54.8	47.4	28.9	27.6	26.0	20.4	17.4	21.4
Germany	57.4	103.1	121.3	193.1	256.1	438.2	322.6	127.2	127.9	116.4	104.4
Greece	6.3	9.3	6.5	4.1	2.7	2.0	0.8	1.3	1.4	1.6	4.2
Ireland	::	::	::	0.1	-	-	0.1	0.4	0.4	1.2	3.9
Italy	11.0	1.4	2.3	4.7	31.7	2.6	1.3	1.8	1.7	0.7	1.4
Luxembourg	0.1	0.0	0.1	0.1	0.2	0.1	0.2	0.2	0.2	0.3	0.4
Netherlands	13.5	7.5	13.9	21.2	21.6	20.3	35.4	52.6	29.3	22.9	34.4
Norway	8.6	6.6	4.4	4.0	4.6	5.2	12.9	3.4	1.5	1.8	2.3
Poland	::	::	::	::	::	::	::	0.6	0.8	3.2	2.9
Portugal	0.2	0.3	0.1	0.1	0.2	0.6	2.1	0.8	0.5	0.3	0.4
Spain	3.7	4.5	4.1	8.6	8.1	11.7	12.6	12.0	5.7	4.7	3.7
Sweden	18.1	19.6	30.0	29.4	27.4	84.0	37.6	18.6	9.0	5.8	9.7
Switzerland	10.9	16.7	24.4	35.8	41.6	18.0	24.7	16.1	17.0	18.0	23.9
United Kingdom	5.9	5.7	16.8	38.2	73.4	32.3	28.0	42.2	55.0	37.0	41.5
United States	26.1	60.7	101.7	73.6	56.3	104.0	144.2	146.5	154.5	128.2	79.8

Source: OECD 1998: 223.

subsequently declared that food would not be provided for Asian migrants (including Indians) unless their countries sent food supplies and medicines in violation of the UN embargo.

While the Iraqi strategy of using its control over migrants for international bargaining is unique thus far, the mere presence of migrants in a country from which they could be expelled has been for some time an element affecting the behavior of the migrants' home countries. Since the late 1970s the countries of South Asia have been aware of their financial dependence upon migration to the Persian Gulf and have recognized that any sudden influx of returning migrants would create a major problem for domestic security, as remittances came to an end, balance-of-payments problems were created, families dependent upon migrant income were threatened with destitution, and large numbers of people were thrown into labor markets where substantial unemployment already existed.

Since the 1990 Gulf War, all these fears have materialized in a variety of world regions. Sending governments aware of these potential consequences have hesitated to criticize host governments for the treatment of migrant workers. When workers have been expelled for strikes and other agitation activities, the home governments have sought to pacify their migrants as well as the host government in an effort to avoid further expulsions. Thus, the understandable reaction of some governments with migrants in Kuwait and Iraq was to see first whether it was possible for their migrants to remain and to assure the security of their citizens, rather than to support international efforts against Iraqi aggression.

A security threat, Robert Jervis has reminded us, is often a matter of perception (Jervis 1976). What are the enemy's capabilities? What are its intentions? A government's assessment of another's intentions with respect both to economic migrants and political refugees is thus critical to how conflictual population movements may become. A government is more likely to accommodate a refugee flow from a neighboring country if it believes the flight is the unfortunate and unintended consequence of a civil conflict than if it believes the flight of the refugees is precisely what is intended. Similarly, a government's response to reports that its citizens abroad are maltreated will depend upon whether it believes that the host country is culpable.

But perception is not everything. As we have seen, there are genuine conflicts of interest among countries on matters of migrants and refugees. Countries quarrel over each other's entry and exit rules, as some countries want those whom another will not let go while some countries force out those whom others do not want. A state's reaction to international population flows can itself be a source of international conflict.

State Responses to Population Movements

How do states react when they are confronted with an unwanted population influx of either economic migrants or refugees? For the foreseeable future the numbers of people who wish to leave or are forced to leave their countries will continue substantially to exceed the numbers that other countries are willing to accept. What strategies are available to states confronted with a rising demand for entrance?

One possible response is to increase immigration. For many observers in industrial countries, migration can be seen as advantageous, providing more young people to offset low national birthrates, manpower for low-wage service-sector jobs that local people do not want, skilled manpower for rapidly growing occupations, and investment by energetic, entrepreneurial newcomers.

But even countries that are relatively open to economic migrants and to refugees will not be able to admit all who want to enter. Sealing borders is one response, but it is rarely wholly effective, even in the case of islands. Control is difficult for any country with large coastlines or land borders. Regulation of employers (including penalties for employing illegal immigrants) and the use of identity cards have made a difference in the countries of Western Europe but are less useful options for a country with large numbers of small firms, a poorly developed administrative structure, and officials who are easily corrupted. Moreover, however opposed the government and the majority of the population are to illegal migration, there are often elements within the society that welcome them: employers, ethnic kinfolk, political sympathizers, or officials willing to accept bribes. Finally, even if a country is able to regulate the number and characteristics of the economic migrants it admits, how can it cope with a massive influx of people in flight from a neighboring country? Faced with unwanted migrants whose entrance they cannot control, governments have increasingly turned to strategies for halting emigration from sending countries. One can identify three such strategies: providing economic assistance, applying political coercion, and using armed intervention.

It has been suggested that an infusion of aid and investment, an improvement in trade, the resolution of a debt crisis, and other measures that would improve income and unemployment in low-income countries would reduce the rate of emigration. Meritorious as these proposals are, there is no evidence that they can reduce emigration in the short run. Indeed, high economic growth rates have often been associated with high rates of emigration. It was so for Great Britain in the nineteenth century and in recent years for South Korea, Turkey, Algeria, and Greece. Only after an extended period of economic growth and a significant rise in wages do we see a substantial reduction in pressures for emigration. Economic aid, however, may not be intended to remedy a country's high unemployment or low economic growth rate, but rather to provide payment to a government to halt a refugee flow.

Assistance can also be used by governments to persuade other countries to retain refugees. The United States and France were willing to provide economic assistance to Thailand if the Thais held Vietnamese refugees rather than permitting them to seek entrance into the United States or France (Rogge 1990: 150–171). The United Nations High Commissioner for Refugees and other international agencies financed largely by the West and Japan provide resources to refugee-receiving countries, especially in Africa, not only as an expression of humanitarian concern but also as a means of enabling refugees to remain in the country of first asylum rather than allowing their movement to advanced industrial countries. International financial support has also been important in inducing refugees to return home when a conflict subsides. Funds for transportation, resettlement, and mine clearance are often critical for a successful, speedy repatriation process.

Second, where generosity does not work or is not financially feasible, receiving countries may employ a variety of threats to halt emigration. Diplomatic pressures, including coercive diplomacy, may be exerted. Throughout the 1990s, substantial bilateral and multilateral efforts at coercive diplomacy were exercised with respect to emigration from the republics of the former Yugoslavia.

During the 1980s, the Indian government pressured the government of Bangladesh to halt Bangladeshi land settlement in the

Chittagong Hill Tracts, which had led local Chakma tribespeople to flee into India. The Indian government is in a position to damage Bangladeshi trade and to affect the flow of rivers if the Bangladeshi government is not accommodating. When Burmese Muslim refugees moved from the Arakan region of Burma into Bangladesh as a result of a Burmese policy of settling non-Muslim Burmese in Arakan, the Bangladeshi government threatened to arm the Burmese Muslim refugees if settlement was not halted. In both cases the threats worked to reduce or temporarily halt the flow (Hazarika 2001).

Coercive diplomacy to induce a country to halt actions that are forcing people to flee may be more effective in combination with collective international sanctions. However, thus far it has been exceedingly difficult for countries burdened by refugee flows to persuade the international community that sanctions should be imposed on the country producing the refugees.

Third, there is the extreme sanction of armed intervention to change the political conditions within the sending country. The 1999 military intervention by NATO, discussed earlier, had the declared goal of reversing the ethnic cleansing of Kosovo by Serb military and paramilitary forces, and offers a clear example of such an event. The Kurdish revolt in Iraq after the Gulf War provides another example of the use of force in dealing with an unwanted refugee flow. As Kurdish refugees entered Turkey, the government of Turkey made clear its unwillingness to add to its own Kurdish population and used its troops to seal the borders. The United States, Great Britain, and other Gulf War allies used their military power to force Iraq to place the Kurdish region under Allied protection. The intervention enabled an estimated 1.5 million Kurds who had fled to Iran and Turkey to return and the Kurds to form their own informal local government.

Finally, a much larger example is offered by the 1971 military intervention by India in what was then East Pakistan. An estimated 10 million refugees fled from East Pakistan to India following the outbreak of a civil war between the eastern and western provinces of Pakistan, a predominately Muslim state whose halves were at opposite sides of the subcontinent. India regarded this refugee flow as the result of a deliberate policy by the Pakistani military to resolve its own internal political problems by forcing East Pakistan's Hindu population into India. Many Indian officials believed that the Pakistani government was seeking to change the demographic balance in favor of West

Pakistan by shifting millions of East Pakistanis to India. The Indian government responded by sending its armed forces into Pakistan; its occupation of East Pakistan forced the partition of the country, and within months India sent the refugees home and the new state of Bangladesh was born.

In each of these instances the high-profile and highly conflictual nature of population movements has affected which institutions make exit and entry rules and engage in international negotiations. Decisions on such matters have come to be dealt with not by ministries of labor, border control officials, or the courts, but at the highest levels of government, in the foreign and defense ministries, the security and intelligence agencies, and by heads of government. The form and intensity of responses to unwanted migrations are themselves indications that such population flows are regarded as threats to security or stability. These responses also suggest that states do not regard refugee flows and emigration as purely internal matters, despite the assertion of the United Nations and other international agencies that countries do not have the right to interfere in the internal affairs of states that produce refugees, even when there is a perceived threat to the security and stability of countries upon whom the burden of unwanted refugees falls.

While the notion of sovereignty is still rhetorically recognized, a variety of "internal" actions by states are increasingly regarded by other states as threats. The spewing of nuclear waste and other hazardous materials into the atmosphere and the contamination of waterways that flow into other countries are no longer regarded as internal matters. In the same spirit, a country that forces its citizens to leave or creates conditions that induce them to leave has internationalized its internal actions.

A conundrum for Western liberal democratic regimes, however, is that they are reluctant to insist that governments restrain the exit of citizens simply because they or others are unwilling to accept them. They believe in the right of emigration by individuals but simultaneously believe that governments retain the right to determine who and how many shall be permitted to enter. Liberal regimes may encourage or even threaten countries that produce refugees and unwanted immigrants in an effort to change the conditions that induce or force people to leave, but they are often reluctant to force people to return home against their will or to press governments to prevent people from leaving. They do not want regimes to prevent political dissidents or persecuted minorities from leaving their country; rather, they want governments to stop their repression.

Advanced industrial countries that admit immigrants prefer an immigration policy that creates the fewest domestic and international political problems. One policy option is to admit those who best satisfy the requirements of the receiving country: those who have skills needed in the labor market, capital to create new businesses, or relatives who would facilitate their integration into the society.[2] But a limited, largely skill-based immigration policy for Western Europe or the United States would still leave large numbers of people banging on the doors, seeking to enter as refugees or, failing that, as illegal immigrants.

An alternative policy based on the needs of immigrants and refugees, though morally more attractive, is more difficult to formulate, more difficult to implement, and legally and politically more contentious. But no policy, short of the obliteration of international boundaries and sovereign states, can deal with the vast numbers of people who want to leave their country for another where opportunities are greater and life is safer. A moral case can be made for giving preference to those in flight, even at the cost of limiting the number of immigrants admitted to meet labor needs or to enable families to reunite. If countries have a ceiling on the number of people they are willing to admit, there is a strong moral argument for providing admission first to those who are persecuted or whose lives are in danger and who have few places to go. But for reasons indicated above, only a narrow definition of what constitutes a refugee, with a case-by-case review, will enable states to put a cap on what they regard as potentially unlimited flows.

As a matter of political realism, then, a significant increase in the flow of refugees or of unwanted illegal economic migrants is likely to lead the governments of population-receiving countries to consider various forms of intervention to change the domestic factors that force or induce people to leave their homeland. If people violate the boundaries of a neighboring country, then they and their government should expect others to intervene in their internal affairs.

Notes

This chapter is based upon Weiner (1996b), with additional materials.

1. The issue was well covered by the press. See, for example, *Agence France Presse*, 16 March 1999 and 21 May 1999; Associated Press, 22 May 1999; *Deutsche Presse-Agentur*, 11 March 1999.
2. For arguments of this type, see Wattenburg and Zinsmeister (1990) and Simon (1981).

— Ten —

IS DEMOGRAPHY DESTINY?

The preceding chapters have considered the powerful demographic changes, in many cases of a type unprecedented in human history, that are currently underway in many countries and regions. Most of these changes impose, or will impose, equally powerful demands upon public and private resources, be they political, social, economic, or moral. This final chapter seeks to draw some cautious conclusions about the extent to which such demands can be expected to have an impact on the security of states, communities, or individuals.

We consider this question in four broad categories: the effects of age-structure changes on established systems of "social security," such as the economic security of the elderly; the implications for military power; the implications of possible demographically driven insecurity in some developing countries, and of possible interstate strife over increasingly scarce resources such as water; and the security implications of recent patterns of ethnic mixing and unmixing, refugee flows, and political responses to them. Our view is primarily from an American perspective, though we do note some aspects that may differ for other Western countries.

Social Insurance/Social Security

For the United States and many other industrialized countries, demographic factors in the past made the present system of "social security" possible. Now changes under way threaten to undermine the social security systems that became nearly universal in such countries during the middle of the twentieth century. In the 1930s, the U.S. Social Security system was created to provide benefits for an elderly population faced with economic hardships during a national depression, and to assure the next generation of a minimal income in old age. The system was initially possible because the age structure of the 1930s U.S. population contained only a small proportion over the statutory retirement age of 65. Its viability was later extended by a "baby boom" (or, in the case of most European countries, a shorter-term "boomlet") at the end of World War II: The large birth cohorts of 1948–1965 meant large labor-force-entrant cohorts during the 1960s to the 1980s, and under the "pay-as-you-go" financing system of Social Security this meant that revenues from Social Security taxes ("contributions") on the working-age population were in excess of the benefits being paid out to the growing population of retired people.

As the baby boom waned—as inevitably it must have done, although this shift appears not to have been adequately anticipated by the Social Security Administration—the youthful age structure that followed the postwar period of high fertility necessarily shifted toward an "older" age distribution. This in turn meant that there would be fewer younger workers contributing to the system and more older recipients, thereby putting into financial jeopardy a system designed on the unsustainable assumption of a more youthful age structure. This purely demographic effect was exacerbated by political decisions during the 1960s and 1970s to sweeten the terms of the Social Security payout; in particular, the effective age for Social Security retirement was lowered, while annual Social Security payments were indexed for inflation using the Consumer Price Index, a statistical measure which many economists believe tended to overstate the real rate of price increases.[1]

Of the many solutions proposed for the financial crisis facing the Social Security system (and the related Medicare system, also threatened by unanticipated demographic changes, along with a failure to control medical costs), most will likely have little impact upon defense and security policies. These include proposals such as reducing the rate of projected increases in Social Security benefits by changing the age at which benefits are provided, and adjusting the cost-of-living increases.

The only real exception is the implicit limitation upon military expenditures that would be required under current laws affecting the Federal budget by proposals to increase Social Security and Medicare taxes. Indeed, more broadly, all entitlement expenditure programs compete with discretionary expenditures on defense, not to mention those on education, social services, and other government programs. Bullets versus benefits will be a continuous issue for the United States, and for many other advanced industrial societies, made worse if these societies feel externally threatened in ways that induce the public, or government leaders, to give greater attention to matters of military security.

The ledger is clearer on the demographic side than on the threat side, and the response to threat is likely to be calls for increased investment in costly military technologies that can provide greater security, particularly against weapons of mass destruction. The intertwining of demography with entitlements ensures continued political debate over defense expenditures.

Military Manpower

Closely linked to this debate is the question of military manpower. It is not simply that the number of young people who might be attracted to military service is declining in advanced industrial societies. In addition, in the United States the military is declining as a prime institution for social mobility, as a strong labor market results in broadening opportunities in education and in other parts of the labor force for previously excluded social groups—women, the poor, and minorities specifically, who had been restricted by virtue of their education or gender. The military continues to attract young people, but retention rates have declined. Trainees, particularly those who acquire technical skills of value in civilian life, can more readily find higher-paid jobs. The military can continue to recruit, but the costs go up as the military finds it necessary to provide its personnel with more benefits, including costly benefits for dependents, in order to compete with the private sector. In other industrialized countries, where youth unemployment rates remain stubbornly high, such patterns are less visible.

Meanwhile, the military is also under political pressure to provide greater security for its own personnel—ironic in the extreme—to make itself more attractive to civilians. Protecting the military has thus become a high priority in the United States and in other advanced industrial societies. More resources will be spent to protect military installations, to protect combat forces, and to limit their use to situations in which personnel losses can be kept to a minimum through costly high-tech operations. Hence the capital intensity of military preparedness seems to be on the rise, just as demand for fiscal resources is also rising to finance the costs of earlier retirement, rising proportions at statutory retirement age, and increasing per-capita health costs.

It is worth noting here that women, as well as previously disadvantaged minorities, are major beneficiaries of slowing population growth rates in developed countries. In one industrial country after another, governments have responded to declining recruitment among young men by seeking to attract and promote young women. The feminization of the military, partly driven by changing attitudes, is also driven by demographic considerations. Moreover, faced with the choice of increasing immigration or providing greater employment opportunities for women, some traditionally conservative social groups that previously favored immigration have more recently opted to encourage female labor force participation. One can see this most dramatically in the oil-producing Gulf States, which have long imported large numbers of workers from Asia to meet the demands for construction and for expanding social services, and which are now seeking local workers; the underutilized female labor force, with its still low labor participation rate, is a natural target for employers. Demography thus drives the feminization of the labor force in economically dynamic, low-fertility countries.

As we have noted throughout this volume, it is difficult to disentangle demographic considerations from the many intervening variables that lie between demography and its consequences. To repeat the obvious, an economy that is growing rapidly and expanding its employment opportunities can cope with rapid population growth more readily than a slow-growing economy. Some countries invest in their future, as it were, by putting resources into mass public education to ensure that the next generation is literate and skilled; others choose to invest in quality education for the upper middle classes. South Korea, Taiwan, and China pursued the former route, India and Pakistan the latter. The empirical evidence suggests that the former has yielded higher economic returns both in per capita incomes and in GNP. If this pattern persists, then one might expect increased disparities not simply between developed and developing countries, but among developing countries, with implications for national economic and political power. Again, one must point to the complexity of factors that shape economic growth, but note that how governments choose to meet the challenges created by demography has implications for their own security.

Demographically Driven Insecurity and Resource Competition

Security issues arise in both urban and rural areas as results of rapid demographic increase. In some developing countries, high rates of population growth in rural areas are followed (often with a lag of two to three decades) by rapid rural-to-urban migration that can produce daunting challenges to creation of necessary infrastructure such as houses, sewerage, potable water, electricity, and transportation. As of 2000, there are some 160 cities in Asia, and 50 in Africa, with a population of a million or more. According to plausible projections, by 2015 there will be more than 20 cities in the developing world with populations that exceed 10 million.

Some security analysts believe these changes imply that future violent conflicts will increasingly take place in urban settings rather than rural or jungle terrain (as in the recent case of Grozny), with substantial implications for military training and tactics (Nichiporuk 2000). Whether or not such urban conflicts transpire, the burgeoning urban populations of the developing world will present significant challenges to their political leaders.

Meanwhile, for other countries the most acute impact of demography on the economic security of populations is on land use, particularly as it affects nomads and herders of cattle. Land use (and land ownership) is a major issue throughout much of Africa, as those who engage in settled agriculture encroach upon those who care for cattle or hunt. Game reserves, the traditional response of colonial governments and of many conservationists, are at risk and everywhere nomadic peoples are driven away from their traditional occupations. Ways of life that persisted for millennia are coming to an end, driven by demography.

There are several important political consequences. One is that we can anticipate more land use disputes in much of Africa and in any places in the Third World where nomadism is ending, settled agriculturalists are seeking land, and land rights are not adequately codified. These disputes often take a particularly vicious form when they coincide with or are made by political entrepreneurs to coincide with ethnic differences. Once land disputes take on an ethnic coloration—based on language, caste, tribe, or whatever label is applied to self-defined communities—they tend to evolve a life of their own independent of the demographic factors that may have been their initial causes. The explanations for why conflicts are initiated are not the same as the explanations for why conflicts persist.

There is also rising concern about competition for resources, not only the classically non-renewable types such as petroleum, but renewable but sometimes regionally scarce resources, such as fresh water. The regions in which such trends appear most disturbing is the arid Middle East and Central Asia, in both of which population growth is reducing the per-capita availability of fresh water in a manner that may make some peoples and states vulnerable to interruption of water supply by other states. Such cases include: the Euphrates region, where the Grand Anatolia project in Turkey will likely reduce water flow to Syria and Iraq by 40 and 80 percent respectively; control by Sudan and other African states of sources of the Nile, essential to sustain the rapidly growing population of Egypt; and the increasing vulnerability of fresh water supplies in the Aral Basin, surrounded by five Central Asian states (formerly Soviet republics) with quite rapid demographic growth rates.[2]

There can be little doubt that real security implications attach to recent patterns of ethnic mixing and unmixing, refugee flows, and political responses to them. Indeed, the decade of the 1990s has been one in which such patterns have been caused by, and have in turn ignited, violent confrontations between military, paramilitary, and civilian groups in diverse settings. From one perspective, ethnically mixed ("diverse") societies represent a positive affirmation of liberal democratic values and contribute to the economic and social advance of societies and regions. This view is strongly supported by some Western elites, especially those of traditional countries of immigration such as the United States, Canada, Australia, and New Zealand. Meanwhile, in other countries (examples are Germany and France) there is less elite consensus on the virtues of ethnic diversity, which some see as a source of persistent friction and a threat to "social peace."

Finally, in some non-liberal but industrialized societies (such as Serbia and Croatia), ethnic mixing is seen as a tangible threat to national identity, and is dealt with by violent efforts at ethnic unmixing, also known as "ethnic cleansing." Such efforts, in both Bosnia and Kosovo, in turn have attracted powerful and violent military intervention by the liberal democracies of NATO, who find such efforts unacceptable and seek to reverse them by force.

Meanwhile, the related flows of refugees and quasi-refugees that are produced by such violent confrontations are often seen by receiving countries as representing deep threats to their own national security. Such perceptions are especially powerful in cases in which such migrations are large and concentrated enough to tilt already delicate ethnic balances (as in Montenegro and Macedonia) or fragile economic and political systems (as in Albania).

Political reactions to such movements, even in liberal democracies, can themselves produce unanticipated perceptions of threat and destabilizing political effects. The electoral success and ultimate entry into government coalition of the Austrian Freedom Party of Jörg Haider in early 2000 was driven in part by public opposition to increasing immigration into Austria, substantially linked to the civil wars in the former Yugoslavia. These Austrian political developments in turn proved to be politically divisive across the 15-state European Union, driven in part by concerns in countries such as Germany and France that this development might legitimize and strengthen their own small right-nationalist party movements.

This political drama was unfolding as this volume was being completed. Its outcome cannot be accurately forecast, but its reality speaks directly to the power of debates about rapid demographic changes—driven by low fertility and accompanied by substantial migration and refugee movements—to spark political turbulence well beyond the national boundaries within which they occur.

Notes

1. In December 1996, a Congressional commission of five leading economists concluded that statistical weaknesses led to an upward bias in the CPI of between 0.8 and 1.6 percent per year, with a central estimate of 1.1 percent. While most economists agreed that there was such an upward bias, there was no consensus as to its magnitude. By March 2000, members of the same commission concluded that statistical improvements since 1996 had lowered such bias to between 0.73 and 0.9 percent, with a central estimate of about 0.8 percent. The subject continues to attract debate among economists and advocates. See, for example, Stevenson (2000).

2. For a more detailed discussion, see Nichiporuk (2000) and Gleick (1993).

REFERENCES

Aleinikoff, Alexander, and Douglas Klusmeyer. 2001. "Plural Nationality: Facing the Future in a Migratory World." In Myron Weiner and Sharon Stanton Russell, eds., *Demography and National Security*. New York: Berghahn Books.

Ascherson, Neal. 1995. *The Black Sea*. New York: Hill and Wang.

Ash, Timothy Garton. 1999. "Cry, the Dismembered Country." *The New York Review of Books*, 14 January, pp. 29–33.

Baiduzhy, Andrei. 1994. "It Is Now a Fact That There is a Demographic Catastrophe in the Country." *Nexavisimaya gazeta*, 16 July: 1(4); translated as "Demographic Disaster: Birth Gap Widens." *Current Digest of the Post-Soviet Press* 46 (28): 8.

Banister, Judith. 2001. "Impacts of Migration to China's Border Regions." In Myron Weiner and Sharon Stanton Russell, eds., *Demography and National Security*. New York: Berghahn Books.

Bell-Fialkoff, Andrew. 1993. "A Brief History of Ethnic Cleansing." *Foreign Affairs* (summer).

Birrell, Robert, and Tanya Birrell. 1981. *An Issue of People: Population and Australian Society*. Melbourne: Longman Cheshire.

Bongaarts, John, and Griffith Feeney. 1998. "On the Quantum and Tempo of Fertility." *Population and Development Review* 24 (2): 271–91.

Brubaker, Rogers. 1989. "Introduction." In Rogers Brubaker, ed., *Immigration and the Politics of Citizenship in Europe and North America*. Lanham, Md: University Press of America.

———. 1993. "Political Dimensions of Migration from and Among Soviet Successor States." In Myron Weiner, ed., *International Migration and Security*. Boulder, Colo.: Westview Press.

———. 1996. *Nationalism Reframed: Nationhood and the National Question in the New Europe*. Cambridge: Cambridge University Press.

Calhoun, John B. 1962. "Population Density and Social Pathology." *Scientific American* (February): 13–146.

Carr-Saunders, A.M. 1936. *World Population: Past Growth and Present Trends*. Oxford: The Clarendon Press.

Chu, Henry. 1999. "Migrants Diluting Tibet Cities." *Los Angeles Times*, 3 August.

Cienski, Jan. 1994. "Russia Faces a Population Crisis." *Deutsche Press-Agentur*, 13 August.

Cocks, Doug. 1996. *People Policy: Australia's Population Choices*. Sydney: University of New South Wales Press.

Connelly, Matthew, and Paul Kennedy. 1994. "Must It Be the Rest Against the West?" *The Atlantic Monthly* (December).

Conquest, R., ed. 1986. *The Last Empire: Nationality and the Soviet Future*. Stanford: Stanford University Press.

Cornelius, Wayne A., Philip L. Martin, and James F. Hollifield, eds. 1994. *Controlling Immigration: A Global Perspective*. Stanford, Calif.: Stanford University Press.

Dalrymple, William. 1998. *From the Holy Mountain: A Journey among the Christians of the Middle East*. New York: Henry Holt.

Debré, R., and A. Sauvy. 1946. *Des Francais pour la France: La probléme de la population*. Paris: Gallimard.

Diamond, Jared. 1997. *Guns, Germs, and Steel: The Fate of Human Societies*. New York and London: W. W. Norton and Co.

Easterlin, Richard A. 1961. "Influences in European Overseas Emigration before World War I." *Economic Development and Cultural Change* 9: 331–51.

Feshbach, Murray. 1979. "Prospects for Outmigration from Central Asia and Kazakhstan in the Next Decade." In *Soviet Economy in a Time of Change*. Washington, D.C.: GPO.

Financial Post. 1994. "Quebec Closes Birth Gap as National Rate Hits Low," 17 November, p. 13.

Gleick, Peter H. 1993. "Water and Conflict: Fresh Water Resources and International Security." *International Security* 18 (1) (summer): 79–112.

Gooderham, Mary. 1995. "Canada Pulling in the Welcome Mat." *San Francisco Chronicle*, 22 March, p. A1.

Gopnik, Adam. 1998. "Streetwise." *The New Yorker*, 8 June, p. 9.

Government of Canada. 1984. "Demographic Aspects of Immigration," report of a meeting, Montreal, 14 December.

Hailbronner, Kay. 1989. "Citizenship and Nationhood in Germany." In Rogers Brubaker, ed., *Immigration and the Politics of Citizenship in Europe and North America*. Lanham, Md: University Press of America.

Hajda, L., and M. Bussinger, eds. 1993. *The Nationalities Factor in Soviet Politics and Society*. New York: Basic Books.

Hatton, Timothy J., and Jeffrey G. Williamson. 1994. "What Drove the Mass Migrations from Europe during the Late Nineteenth Century?" *Population and Development Review* 20 (3): 533–59.

Haub, Carl. 1994. "Population Change in the Former Soviet Republics." *Population Bulletin* 49 (4): 13, Table A-3.

Hauser, Philip M. 1965. "Demographic Dimensions of World Politics." In Larry K. Y. Ng, ed., *The Population Crisis*. Bloomington: Indiana University Press.

Hazarika, Sanjoy. 2001. "A Question of Outsiders: Bangladesh, Myanmar, and Bhutan." In Myron Weiner and Sharon Stanton Russell, eds., *Demography and National Security*. New York: Berghahn Books.

Henry, Louis. 1961. "Some Data on Natural Fertility." *Eugenics Quarterly* 8 (2): 81–91.

Hoffmann, Stanley. 1994. "France: Keeping the Demons at Bay." *New York Review of Books* XLI(5): 14.

Hovy, Bela, and Hania Zlotnik. 1994. "Europe without Internal Frontiers and International Migration." *Population Bulletin of the United Nations* 36: 19–42.

Huntington, Samuel P. 1996. *The Clash of Civilizations and the Remaking of World Order*. New York: Simon and Schuster.

Jervis, Robert. 1976. *Perception and Misperception in International Politics*. Princeton: Princeton University Press.

Jones, Ellen, and Fred W. Grupp. 1987. *Modernization, Value Change, and Fertility in the Soviet Union*. Cambridge: Cambridge University Press.

Kaufmann, Chaim. 1996a. "Possible and Impossible Solutions to Ethnic Civil Wars." *International Security* 20 (4): 136–75.

———. 1996b. "Intervention in Ethnic and Ideological Civil Wars: Why One Can Be Done and the Other Can't." *Security Studies* 6 (1): 62–103.

———. 1998. "When All Else Fails: Ethnic Population Transfers and Partitions in the Twentieth Century." *International Security* 23 (2): 120–156.

Kennedy, Paul M. 1994. *Preparing for the Twenty-first Century*. New York: Vintage Books.

Keynes, J. M. 1937. "The Economic Consequences of a Declining Population." *Eugenics Review* 29: 13–17.

Kristof, Nicholas D. 1999. "A Sexy Economic Feud of No Interest to the I.M.F.." *New York Times*, 17 June, p. A4.

Kulischer, Eugene M. 1948. *Europe on the Move: War and Population Changes, 1917–47.* New York: Columbia University Press.

Lesthaeghe, Ron, and Paul Willems. 1999. "Is Low Fertility a Temporary Phenomenon in the European Union?" *Population and Development Review* 25 (2): 211–28.

Levesque, René. 1968. "The Snare of Biculturalism." In R. Levesque, ed., *An Option for Quebec.* Toronto: McClelland and Stewart.

Lines, William J. 1992. *Taming the Great South Land: A History of the Conquest of Nature in Australia.* Sydney: Allen and Unwin.

Lutz, Wolfgang. 1994. "The Future of World Population." *Population Reference Bureau* (June) 49 (1): 17.

M2 Presswire. 1996. 19 January; 28 May.

———. 1997. 16 January.

Marchant, James, ed. 1920. *Problems of Population and Parenthood.* London: Chapman and Hall.

Marrus, Michael. 1985. *The Unwanted: European Refugees in the Twentieth Century.* New York: Oxford University Press.

Massey, Douglas S., et al. 1993. "Theories of International Migration: A Review and Appraisal." *Population and Development Review* 19: 431–66.

———. 1994. "International Migration Theory: The North American Case." *Population and Development Review* 20: 699–751.

Meyer, Herbert E. 1978. "The Coming Soviet Ethnic Crisis." *Fortune,* 14 August.

Migration News. 1994. "IOM Reports on Trafficking, Transit Migration." University of California, Davis. <http://migration.ucdavis.edu> (November).

———. 1998. "Germany: SPD Wins." University of California, Davis. <http://migration.ucdavis.edu> (October).

Mitchell, B. R. 1980. *European Historical Statistics, 1750–1975.* 2nd rev. ed. New York: N.Y. Facts on File.

Morris, B. 1987. *The Birth of the Palestinian Refugee Problem, 1947–1949.* Cambridge: Cambridge University Press.

Moskva. 1986. Editor's Foreword.

Myrdal, Gunnar. 1940. *Population: A Problem for Democracy.* Reprinted 1962. Gloucester, Mass.: Peter Smith.

New Yorker. 1994. "This is War," 21 February, p. 6.

Nichiporuk, Brian. 2000. *The Security Dynamics of Demographic Factors.* Santa Monica, Calif.: RAND, Document MR-1088-WFHF/RF/DLPF/A.

OECD. 1998. *SOPEMI: Trends in International Migration, Annual Report.* 1998 ed. Paris: OECD.

Rager, F. A. 1941. "Japanese Emigration and Japan's 'Population Pressure.'" *Pacific Affairs* (September): 300–21.

Raspail, Jean. 1995. *The Camp of the Saints.* Petosky, Mich.: The Social Contract Press.

Rogge, John P. 1990. "Thailand's Refugee Policy: Some Thoughts on Its Origin and Future Direction." In Howard Adelman and C. Michael Lanphier, eds., *Refuge or Asylum.* Toronto: York Lane Press.

Rubinstein, Alvin Z., ed. 1983. *The Great Game: Rivalry in the Persian Gulf and South Asia.* New York: Praeger.

Russell, Sharon Stanton. 1993. *International Migration in North America, Europe, Central Asia, the Middle East and North Africa: Research and Research-Related Activities.* Geneva: Economic Commission for Europe and the World Bank, pp. 23 and 81.

———. 1995. "International Migration: Implications for the World Bank, Human Resources Development and Operations Policy." Working Paper Number 54. Washington, D.C.: The World Bank (May).

Russell, Sharon Stanton, Charles B. Keely, and Bryan P. Christian. 2000. "Multilateral Diplomacy to Harmonize Asylum Policy in Europe: 1984–1993." Washington,

D.C.: Georgetown University, Institute for the Study of International Migration, forthcoming. Working Paper.

Safire, William. 1993. "On Language." *The New York Times Sunday Magazine*, 14 March, p. 24.

Sauvy, A. 1981. "Population Changes: Contemporary Models and Theories." *Research in Population and Economics* 3: 234.

Simon, Julian L. 1981. *The Economic Consequences of Immigration*. New York: Basil Blackwell.

Smith, James P,. and Barry Edmonston, eds. 1997. *The New Americans: Economic, Demographic, and Fiscal Effects of Immigration*. Washington, D.C.: National Academy Press.

Stevenson, Richard W. 2000. "Economists Readjust Estimate of Overstatement of Inflation." *New York Times*, 1 March, p. C14.

Strangeland, Charles E. 1904. *Pre-Malthusian Doctrines of Population: A Study in the History of Economic Theory*. Reprinted 1966. New York: Kelley.

Szporluk, R. 1989. "Dilemmas of Russian Nationalism." *Problems of Communism* (July–August).

Taylor, Charles, et al. 1994. *Multiculturalism: Examining the Politics of Recognition*. Princeton, N.J.: Princeton University Press.

Teitelbaum, Michael S. 1978. "Aging Populations." In *Encyclopædia Britannica Yearbook 1978*. New York: Encyclopædia Britannica.

——— . 1987. Review of *The Birth Dearth*. *Congressional Record* 133 (125), 28 July.

———. 1988. "Demographic Change Through the Lenses of Science and Politics." *Proceedings of the American Philosophical Society* 132 (2): 173–84.

———. 1992. "Advocacy, Ambivalence, Ambiguity: Immigration Policy and Prospects in the United States." *Proceedings of the American Philosophical Society* 136: 208–25.

———. 2001. "International Migration: Predicting the Unknowable." In Myron Weiner and Sharon Stanton Russell, eds., *Demography and National Security*. New York: Berghahn Books.

Teitelbaum, Michael S., and Sharon Stanton Russell. 1994. "International Migration, Fertility, and Development." In Robert Cassen and contributors, *Population and Development: Old Debates, New Conclusions*. New Brunswick, N.J. and Oxford: Island Press.

Teitelbaum, Michael S., and Jay M. Winter. 1985. *The Fear of Population Decline*. Orlando, Fla. and London: Academic Press.

———. 1998. *A Question of Numbers: High Migration, Low Fertility, and the Politics of National Identity*. New York: Hill and Wang.

The Economist. 1999. "Both Turkish and German?" 6 February, U.S. ed., p. S12.

Thucydides. *The Peleponnesian War*. New York: Modern Library [1934].

Tirtosudarmo, Riwanto. 2001. "Demography and Security: Transmigration Policy in Indonesia." In Myron Weiner and Sharon Stanton Russell, eds., *Demography and National Security*. New York: Berghahn Books.

Turner, Craig. 1995. "Quebec Separatism Brings Fear of Intolerance." *Los Angeles Times*, 10 November, p. A10.

United Nations. 1999. *World Population Prospects: The 1998 Revision*. Vol. 1: Comprehensive Tables. United Nations Department of Economic and Social Affairs, Population Division.

———. 2000. *Replacement Migration: Is It a Solution to Declining and Ageing Populations?* New York: United Nations. ESA/P/WP.160.

U.S. Committee for Refugees. 2000. *World Refugee Survey 2000*. Washington, D.C.: Immigration and Refugee Services of America.

Varshney, Ashutosh. 2001. *Civic Life and Ethnic Conflict: Hindus and Muslims in India*. New Haven: Yale University Press (forthcoming).

Vishnevsky, A. 1993. "Ideologized Demography." Paper presented at the Bellagio Conference on Migration, Fertility, and National Identity (June). Originally published in Russian in *Herald of the USSR Academy of Sciences* (1991) 10: 2–180.

Wallace, James N. 1977. "In USSR, Minority Problems Just Won't Wither Away." *U.S. News and World Report*, 14 February.

Washington *Post*. 1994a. "Invade Haiti?" Editorial, 8 June, p. A22.

———. 1994b. "Zhirinovsky's Population Plan: To Father a Child per Region," 10 September, p. A16.

Wattenberg, Ben J. 1987. *The Birth Dearth: What Happens When People in Free Countries Don't Have Enough Babies?* 2nd ed., 1989. New York: Pharos Books.

Wattenburg, Ben J., and Karl Zinsmeister. 1990. "The Case for More Immigration." *Commentary* 89: 4.

Weil, Patrick. 1998. "The State Matters: Immigration Control in Developed Countries." Preliminary unedited version prepared for Population Division, Department of Economic and Social Affairs, United Nations ESA/P/WP/146. New York: United Nations, p. 18.

Weiner, Myron. 1971. "Political Demography: An Inquiry into the Political Consequences of Population Change." In *Rapid Population Growth: Consequences and Policy Implications*. National Academy of Science, Office of the Foreign Secretary. Baltimore: Johns Hopkins University Press.

———. 1978. *Sons of the Soil: Migration and Ethnic Conflict in India*. Princeton: Princeton University Press.

Weiner, Myron, ed. 1993. *International Migration and Security*. Boulder: Westview Press.

———. 1995. *The Global Migration Crisis: Challenge to States and to Human Rights*. New York: HarperCollins College Publishers.

———. 1996a. "A Security Perspective on International Migration." *The Fletcher Forum on World Affairs* 20 (2): 17–34.

———. 1996b. "Bad Neighbors, Bad Neighborhoods: An Inquiry into the Causes of Refugee Flows." *International Security* 21 (1) (summer): 5–42.

Weiner, Myron, and Michael S. Teitelbaum, eds. 1995. *Threatened Peoples, Threatened Borders: Migration and U.S. Foreign Policy*. New Jersey: W. W. Norton.

Weiner, Myron, and Sharon Stanton Russell, eds. 2001. *Demography and National Security*. New York: Berghahn Books.

Westoff, Charles F., and Elise F. Jones. 1979. "The End of 'Catholic' Fertility." *Demography* 16 (2): 209–17.

Winter, J. M. 1994. "Le massacre des Arméniens." *Le Monde*, 3 August.

Wohlstetter, Albert. 1994. "Creating a Greater Serbia." *New Republic* 211 (5) (1 August): 22.

Zolberg, Aristide R. 1998. "Matters of State: Theorizing Immigration Policy." In Noah M. J. Pickus, ed., *Immigration and Citizenship in the Twenty-first Century*. Lanham, Md.: Rowman and Littlefield.

INDEX